NOT FORGOTTEN

GEORGE WEIGEL

NOT FORGOTTEN

Elegies for, and Reminiscences of,
a Diverse Cast of Characters,
Most of Them Admirable

IGNATIUS PRESS   SAN FRANCISCO

Cover Photos
(*Credits on page 222*)
1st Row: Bernardin Gantin, Daniel Patrick Moynihan, Cass Elliot, R. Sargent Shriver
2nd Row: Charles W. Colson, Lindy Boggs, Don J. Briel, Tom Wolfe
3rd Row: James H. Billington, Tycho Brahe, Pete Seeger, Herman Wouk
4th Row: Avery Dulles, S.J.; Hugh Dowding; Francis X. Ford, M.M.; Aaron Jean-Marie Lustiger
5th Row: James V. Schall, S.J.; Pope Saint John Paul II; Charles Krauthammer; Henry M. Jackson
6th Row: Albert Einstein; Francis Eugene George, O.M.I.; William F. Buckley, Jr.; Leszek Kołakowski
7th Row: Cokie Roberts, Peter L. Berger, Michael Novak, Václav Havel
8th Row: Jackie Robinson, Henry J. Hyde, Anwar Sadat, Franz Jägerstätter

Cover design by John Herreid

© 2020 by Ignatius Press, San Francisco
All rights reserved
ISBN 978-1-62164-415-6 (PB)
ISBN 978-1-64229-153-7 (eBook)
Library of Congress Catalogue number 2020946184
Printed in the United States of America ∞

For Bryn and John
(and William, Claire, and Lucy)

CONTENTS

NOT FORGOTTEN

PREFACE

When a practitioner of the weekly newspaper column and the occasional essay enters the authorial lists at age twenty-eight, as I did in 1979, he begins to notice something when he hits fifty-five or sixty: a lot more elegiac columns and essays are flowing, more or less naturally, from his keyboard. Parents, old friends, mentors, heroes, and villains who made an impression—all seem to be leaving the scene at an accelerating rate (not unlike the flow of time itself). The elegies follow in due course.

This collection of reminiscences and obituaries—most of them involving people I've had the good fortune to know, others whom I've only known at a distance or through a lifelong fascination with history and biography, and one a spacecraft—is a byproduct of that acceleration of elegiac writing I noticed myself doing as the twenty-first century entered its second decade. Perhaps, I thought, some of the tributes and reminiscences I'd written previously, as well as those of more recent vintage, might have lasting value for the insight these lives, most of them admirable, give us into the human and Christian condition today.

The sketches herein are of varying length and depth; the longitudinal variations have little to do with the magnitude or historical impact of the characters in question and everything to do with the formats in which they were originally written. Many of them began as weekly newspaper columns in the Catholic press. Others were published by secular newspapers and magazines, in both print and online formats; one was written for a memorial book. The reminiscences of my father and mother were delivered as reflections at their Masses of Christian Burial. I've taken the liberty of polishing each piece a bit but without, I hope, losing their original flavor.

It's a rather diverse cast of characters, and the people about whose lives I have chosen to write inevitably reflect my own history, personal debts, and interests. A few of those herein lived a very long time ago. Most shared at least some of my life span and, like me, they wrestled with the profound changes that have come to both Church and world since 1951. Yet I believe there's a common thread weaving its way across the centuries and through this patchwork quilt of personalities: each of the people I've memorialized has something to teach us today about righteous and noble living—although a few of them teach those lessons along the old *via negativa*.

That is why they are "not forgotten" and shouldn't be. Each wove his or her life story into the tapestry of the human adventure. And therefore, as Mrs. Loman said in *Death of a Salesman*, "attention must be paid." From my point of view as a Catholic thinker and writer, I also have found in many of these lives marvelous examples of what the author of the Letter to the Hebrews calls "so great a cloud of witnesses" (12:1) who, despite their exit from the terrestrial stage, remain our companions on the journey to the New Jerusalem and the Wedding Feast of the Lamb.

And that is even more reason to remember—and to give thanks for what I've learned from those about whom I've written after their deaths.

The Critical Arabist

Fouad Ajami (1945–2014)

The death of Middle East scholar Fouad Ajami on June 22, 2014, was a devastating blow to hopes for an intelligent debate about the volatile Levant and the U.S. role in it. For decades, Fouad, a man of genius, was an invaluable mentor in matters involving the Arab world and its often-lethal discontents. It was a cauldron of self-destructive passions he knew well, this Lebanese Shiite who came to the United States because he found in America a model of the civility and tolerance he wished for his people.

Fouad Ajami described the pathologies of the Arab world with clarity and singular literary grace. His was not the carping of the exile who despises what he has left behind; it was the sharp, penetrating, and ultimately compassionate (because true) critique of one who mourned the catastrophic condition of contemporary Arab civilization; who deplored the hijacking of Arab politics by self-serving dictators, virulent anti-Semites, and Islamist fanatics; and who felt a deep pity for the untold numbers of lives warped or lost in consequence. That moral passion about the corruptions of Arab culture was never more eloquently expressed than in the column Fouad wrote for the *Wall Street Journal* a month after 9/11:

> A darkness, a long winter, has descended on the Arabs. Nothing grows in the middle between an authoritarian political order and populations given to perennial flings with dictators, abandoned to their most malignant hatreds. Something is amiss in an Arab world that besieges American embassies for visas and at the same time celebrates America's calamities. Something has gone terribly wrong in a world where young men strap themselves with explosives, only to be hailed as "martyrs" and "avengers."

In early 2014, I got an email from Fouad, expressing his enthusiasm for what he had seen of Pope Francis and teasing me that, under these circumstances, he might become a Catholic. It was a lighthearted comment with a serious undertone. For years, Fouad had told me of his respect for John Paul II and Benedict XVI; he had also invited me to address his seminar at the Johns Hopkins University School of Advanced International Studies on the role of the Catholic Church in shaping world politics. That role, Fouad understood, had changed. The power the Church deployed today was not the political power it once wielded; it was now moral power, the power of persuasion and reason, both of which Fouad believed essential to the Arab world's recovery from the intellectual morass into which it had sunk centuries ago.

Thus, while the herd of independent minds in the global media was having a field day condemning Benedict XVI for his 2006 Regensburg lecture, Fouad understood that the Bavarian pope had correctly identified the two critical challenges that contemporary history posed to twenty-first-century Islam: the challenges of finding, within authoritative Islamic sources, Islamic warrants underwriting religious tolerance and distinguishing religious and political authority in public life.

The answer to political Islamism and jihadism, Fouad knew, was not turning hundreds of millions of Muslims into good secular liberals; that simply wasn't going to happen, the fantasies of foreign policy strategists and commentators notwithstanding. But there was an alternative. The Catholic Church had retrieved lost elements of its own tradition and learned some new things along the way, in its wrestling with religious freedom and political modernity. That's what Islam would have to do.

Fouad Ajami would have been heartbroken over Mosul being emptied of its Christians by the homicidal maniacs of the *soi-disant* Islamic State of Iraq and the Levant. The Middle East he longed to help bring to birth was a region that would honor its many religious traditions and cherish the cultural gifts each faith offered its neighbors. The incomprehensible carelessness of Americans in washing their hands of Iraq in the years immediately before his death deeply saddened him. So, I expect, did the tendency of Christian leaders in the Middle East to curry favor with whatever dictator happened to be in power, in the vain hope that their communities would be left alone. That was strategic folly, Fouad knew, because it helped empower the criminals and the haters.

May the great soul of this man of reason and decency be an everlasting memory and an inspiration to others.

Hearing Rumors of Angels
Peter L. Berger (1929–2017)

They left the stage in pairs: Cardinal Avery Dulles, S.J., in 2008 and Father Richard John Neuhaus in 2009; Michael Novak in 2017 and then, four months later, on June 27, 2017, Peter Berger—men whose work I had first read as an undergraduate and who later became friends and colleagues in a variety of enterprises. It's a strange feeling, having been for decades the junior subaltern; now, increasingly, something of an elder. But what a preparation I was fortunate enough to have been given, first by these men's books, then by our conversation, collaboration, and friendship. Their generosity to young people eager to join their ranks is a gift I shall never forget, and one I hope I've learned to emulate.

I read a lot of Berger in college—*Invitation to Sociology, The Social Construction of Reality, Movement and Revolution* (coauthored with Neuhaus, then in his rabble-rouser, radical period), and *A Rumor of Angels*; the last, with its intriguing analysis of how everyday life sends out "signals of transcendence" that can open us to religious faith (or simply to a less-flattened, more capacious worldview) is a small gem on which I still rely in lectures and articles today, more than four decades later. I first met Berger during the founding days of the Institute on Religion and Democracy, which Peter helped launch along with the rest of the Catholic (or about-to-be Catholic) neocon suspects and a handful of evangelical Protestants tired of their denominations' drift into mindless (and antibiblical) leftism, theologically and politically. But it was not until the late spring of 1988 that I spent any significant time with Peter Berger. And what a time it was.

Peter had a generous grant from a well-known conservative foundation and proposed to use the remainder of it to take Neuhaus, Novak, and me with him to Rome for a week, to engage Vatican officials in conversation about John Paul II's 1987 social encyclical, *Sollicitudo Rei Socialis* (The Church's Social Concern), which had caused all of us some, well, concerns. The arrangements he made were first-rate, for as Berger often put it, "I am prepared to test the outer limits of the exotic in any culture in which I find myself, but I don't like surprises before breakfast"—so we stayed atop Monte Mario at the five-star Cavalieri Hilton (now the Rome Cavalieri Waldorf Astoria). This headquarters for our expedition necessitated expensive cab rides to our Roman destinations but, *pace* Peter's wishes, the Cavalieri guaranteed that there were no shockers *prima della prima collazione*.

I was a complete neophyte as a Vaticanista in those days, and I suppose we were all a bit shocked by the languid pace of the Roman Curia and the crotchetiness of even its mid-tier officials when friendly queries were raised about their arguments and claims. Later, I was to learn that John Paul II was as dissatisfied with the Curia's work on what became *Sollicitudo Rei Socialis* as we were, a story I would later recount in the first volume of my biography of the Pope, *Witness to Hope*. In any event, the experience was an invaluable one in introducing me to the ways of the Magic Kingdom on the Tiber and its denizens.

Perhaps the most memorably Bergeresque moment of our week came as we were waiting in a badly lit and poorly decorated parlor outside the principal office of Cardinal Joseph Ratzinger, prefect of the Congregation for the Doctrine of the Faith, "formerly known as the Inquisition", as reporters of a certain cast of mind never fail to remind us. The parlor included an unattractive painting of some historical scene or other—not, I hasten to add, the use of thumbscrews on heretics during the Counter-Reformation—and that nondescript picture initiated me into the world of Peter Berger's robust sense of humor, which often combined deep historical knowledge with a whimsical view of the human condition. As we were all sitting, a bit awestruck, in the great Ratzinger's antechamber, Peter said out of nowhere, "This room reminds me of a medieval dentist's office. And speaking of dentists, look at that awful painting and remind yourself that, in any historical painting depicting a scene prior to the mid-nineteenth century, 80 percent of the people in the picture are suffering severe toothache." Delivered in Peter's inimitably Viennese accent, a souvenir of the city of his birth, that droll observation had us all laughing just before Ratzinger came out and greeted us—and later made the intriguing observation that *Sollicitudo Rei Socialis* was "not our [meaning his congregation's] work".

Peter Berger had a remarkable gift for intellectual curiosity and an admirable willingness to admit that he was, on occasion, wrong. Thus, the sociologist who was once at the forefront of secularization theory (the claim that modernization inevitably involves radical and deep secularization) later came to admit that he'd had it wrong—and, indeed, that the secularization hypothesis had been empirically falsified everywhere in a world that was becoming more, not less, intensely religious, except for that outlier known as Western Europe. The American experience of hypermodernization combined with intense religiosity had something to do with Peter's change of mind on this point and led him to coin the immortal epigram "The United States is a nation of Indians [the most intensely religious nation on earth] ruled by an elite of Swedes [the world's most secular nation]."

In another intellectual journey that might once have surprised him, had anyone predicted it in the early 1960s, Berger, with his respect for data, came to understand the importance of entrepreneurship, enterprise, and markets in giving the Third World the tools with which to lift itself out of misery and poverty. But he was never a romantic about capitalism, knew that economic development involved disruptive cultural costs, and was always sensitive to what Reinhold Niebuhr would have called the inevitable tragedies of history in an imperfect world. Berger was fascinated by Asia, hoped that Malaysia and Indonesia might provide models of a modernizing Islam liberated from the pathologies of the Arab Middle East, and maintained an extraordinarily wide range of contacts with scholars, businesspeople, and activists all over the Third World. Their common bond was a willingness to think outside the box about political and economic development while always keeping in mind the cultural preconditions necessary to make free politics and free economics work.

My last two extended experiences with Peter—in Berlin in December 2007 and in Boston in April 2015—gave me an even deeper appreciation of his insatiable curiosity and his commitment to intellectual ecumenism. In Berlin, he gathered a divergent crew of intellectuals to try to beat some sense into German social democrats about religion and society (meaning, in the main, to deprogram them from their conviction that religiously informed public moral argument was always bad news in a democracy). I don't think we made much headway, but it wasn't because of Peter's indefatigable good humor, intellectual energy, and language skills. In Boston, a similarly across-the-ideological-board cast of characters spent three sharp-edged days under Peter's direction, exploring the ways in which various religious communities and cultures coped (or didn't cope) with late modernity and postmodernity. (My paper at that conference eventually grew into a book, *The Irony of Modern Catholic History*.) Like his longtime friend Neuhaus, Berger was a masterful conference chairman, always asking the probing question that kept everyone on their toes and thinking outside their accustomed intellectual comfort zones. That he pulled off the Boston conference while confined to a wheelchair demonstrated that his physical courage matched his intellectual boldness.

Peter's marriage to fellow sociologist Brigitte Kellner, herself a distinguished scholar (and survivor of a Nazi concentration camp), was one of the greatest I've ever witnessed. And in the two years left to him after Brigitte's death in 2015, Peter's first response to my telephonic inquiries about how he was doing was always the same: he spoke of how much he missed his wife. But then we moved on to the other staple of our conversation, the exchange of new jokes we had heard. I have known some great storytellers, but I have rarely met anyone who reveled in jokes as much as Peter did—especially jokes that ethnic or national groups told about themselves, thereby revealing (wittingly or not) some of their deepest characteristics.

He had a deeply Lutheran view of the world and of life; there was no "Brother Sun, Sister Moon" happy-talk piety in Peter Ludwig Berger. But his fondness for jokes and his delight in sharing them suggested that, at bottom, he knew that it's all a divine comedy, whatever the chiaroscuro shadings.

A Christian Gentleman in Washington
James H. Billington (1929–2018)

There have been only fourteen Librarians of Congress since the position was created by law in 1802—and then immediately filled by President Thomas Jefferson with his former campaign manager, the otherwise unmemorable John J. Beckley. Since then, the Library of Congress has been led by a variety of characters who brought to the job various qualifications, some of them as slim as Mr. Beckley's. But whatever their qualifications or length of tenure, none of them had a greater impact on the Library or did more to make it an integral part of the nation's cultural life than James H. Billington, who served as Librarian from 1987 until 2015 and died three years later at age eighty-nine.

Billington's service transformed the Library in several ways. After renovating its first and greatest structure, he turned the glorious Thomas Jefferson Building into a kind of national exhibit space; there, he taught America things it may not have known about itself (as in the 1998 exhibit *Religion and the Founding of the American Republic*) and quietly challenged some of the regnant shibboleths of hypersecularist scholarship by mounting exhibitions like *Rome Reborn: The Vatican Library and Renaissance Culture*, which illustrated the profound impact of religious conviction on the Renaissance (and vice versa). An otherwise admiring *Washington Post* obituary repeated the canard that Billington had "struggled" to adjust to the digital age. That was nonsense. The truth of the matter is that Jim Billington launched the Library of Congress into the digital age, insisting that its collections be made available online and making the Library the hub of an international consortium of national libraries whose purpose was to build global solidarity and a global conversation by making knowledge available to anyone, anywhere.

He created the Kluge Center at the Library, so that visiting scholars could work on site with its vast resources, and the Kluge Prize for Lifetime Achievement in the Human Sciences—filling a gap of which Alfred Nobel was evidently unaware, but matching the Swedish inventor's generosity. In partnership with First Lady Laura Bush, Billington created the annual National Book Festival. And he didn't neglect popular culture, helping to create the Gershwin Prize for Popular Song and the Packard Campus for Audio-Visual Conservation in Culpepper, Virginia, for preserving audiovisual materials, including classic American films. To make all this possible, he used his formidable skills as a fundraiser to bring hundreds of millions of dollars to Library projects from private sector philanthropy.

Throughout his life, however, Jim Billington was always a teacher. He was much admired by the undergraduates he taught and the graduate students he guided at Harvard and Princeton. When, as Librarian, he accompanied a CODEL (Congressional Delegation, in swamp-speak) to a Russia whose cultural history he understood as well as anyone in the West, the solons were given a challenging and engaging seminar, not a junket. He did the same for President and Mrs. Reagan prior to and during their historic visit to Moscow in 1988. During the years that he led the Woodrow Wilson International Center for Scholars, he displayed a remarkable capacity to enter any conversation among high-powered (and often high-ego) academics and ask the kind of questions that got everyone thinking about the subject matter at hand in a new way. And at the Wilson Center, as during his later work at the Library of Congress, he deftly made sure that theology was welcome in the world of scholarship.

In 1984–1985, when I had the privilege of being a Wilson Center fellow, the nation's official memorial to its twenty-eighth president was housed in the upper floors of the old Smithsonian Castle, right on the National Mall. Designed by that great architectural copycat James Renwick, the Castle was modeled on a medieval Norman monastery. Its common refectory for fellows and staff, the cell-like offices we used, and the cramped library all contributed to giving the place a monastic atmosphere—not in the sense of an escape from the world, but as a quiet place where the world could be brought into focus by careful thinking and vibrant conversation, often based on great texts. In that distinctive environment, Jim

Billington presided over a scholarly community much as one imagines an abbot like Suger of Saint-Denis or Bernard of Clairvaux might have done: by making sure that everyone appreciated the opportunities that the venue presented for serious reflection, and by insisting that everyone keep asking the right questions, which were often the unexpected or hard questions.

That was entirely appropriate, because James Hadley Billington was, above all, a Christian gentleman. There aren't many of them around anymore and the United States is the poorer for it. But he was certainly one. Whether focused on Russia or the history of revolutionary thought or the meaning of icons, his scholarship was permeated by the convictions that human beings were theotropic, ordered to God by some sort of hardwiring, and that if the true God were not known and worshipped, false gods surely would be. Jim Billington cast his spiritual lot with the God of the Bible, whom he knew through Christian faith and the Episcopal Church, and that shaped everything else about him: his family life, his thought, and his public service. His was an old-school sort of Anglicanism and much the better for it. For like his fellow historian Jaroslav Pelikan, Billington understood that, while traditionalism is the dead faith of the living, tradition is the living faith of the dead—and the twenty-first-century Christian's point of contact over millennia with some of the greatest of human spirits.

Some may have found his style more aristocratic than has been common in Washington since the days when Dean Acheson presided over the Department of State with his Guardsman's mustache, his natty, three-piece suits, and his disdain for "the primitives". But over the thirty years of our friendship, I was constantly struck by another of Jim Billington's strengths: there was not a scintilla of snobbery about the man. In him, an aristocracy of the intellect coexisted with a democracy of the heart, in that he wanted everyone to be able to share the treasures of knowledge and understanding that meant so much to him—especially those who bore responsibility for the common good in these United States. His children fondly called him the "Weapon of Mass Instruction", and with good reason.

The day after he died, this Catholic found himself praying Psalm 24 in the Church's daily order of worship, the Liturgy of the Hours, and thinking of Jim Billington:

Who shall climb the mountain of the Lord?
Who shall stand in his holy place?
The man with clean hands and pure heart,
who desires not worthless things,
who has not sworn so as to deceive his neighbor.
He shall receive blessings from the Lord
and reward from the God who saves him.

The capital of a great power, like Washington, D.C., is not usually replete with clean-handed and pure-hearted men, so we should appreciate them when they appear. James H. Billington was such a man. And while I am confident that he has received blessings from the Lord, I hope that the nation's capital and its contentious denizens know what a blessing he was to it, and to them, for so many years.

Mother-Daughter Act

Lindy Boggs (1916–2013) and
Cokie Roberts (1943–2019)

Alas, none of the many encomia to Cokie Roberts, the NPR and ABC commentator and "Washington insider" who died of cancer on September 17, 2019, resurrected her single greatest line—which actually had a bit of an influence on the world of affairs. It involved her mother, Lindy Boggs; the Clintons; the culture wars; and the Vatican—and it's worth recalling amidst the other celebrations of Cokie Roberts' life and accomplishments. Remembering it also affords an opportunity to pay tribute to Lindy, who died in 2013, for she deserves remembrance and celebration at least as much as her more famous daughter.

The story begins in Washington in 1997. The newly reelected Clinton administration was furious with the Vatican for the Holy See's role in derailing Clintonista plans to have abortion-on-demand declared a universal human right at the 1994 Cairo International Conference on Population and Development and the 1995 Beijing Fourth World Conference on Women. Payback was in order. And while an overt assault on Pope John Paul II was understood to be imprudent, even among the feminist ideologues in the East Wing, there were other means of registering displeasure. So the chosen vehicle for Clintonian retribution became the U.S. embassy to the Holy See.

Standard diplomatic practice calls for the sending state (in this case, the U.S.) to quietly vet its potential nominee for ambassador with the receiving entity (in this case, the Holy See). Twice, the Clintons proposed nominees calculated to express the Clintons' (and especially Hillary's) contempt: if memory serves, one was a triple-divorcee, and the other was an ex-nun then involved in state politics. The Vatican did not kowtow to bullies in those days, so Holy See officials quietly

explained that, as neither nominee was acceptable, and a public dec-
laration of *persona non grata* blocking the acceptance of either would
embarrass all concerned, the administration should try again.

Plan C, for Team Clinton, came down to this: All right, if you
don't want people who we think can do the job, we'll give you
an eighty-one-year-old former Member of Congress—Lindy Boggs.
Take that, Your Holiness.

Lindy was not enthusiastic about the appointment, having settled into retirement after nine terms in the House of Representatives
(where in 1973 she had succeeded her late husband, former majority
leader Hale Boggs). So she told daughter Cokie that she was going to
decline. To which Cokie replied, "C'mon, Mom, it's the two things
you like doing best in the world—going to Mass and going to parties."

Lindy accepted.

Shortly after her confirmation, Lindy and I ran into each other in
Rome, where I was working on the first volume of my John Paul II
biography, *Witness to Hope*. She was visiting the Pontifical North
American College for a dinner in the student kitchen on the college's
rooftop, hosted by then-New Orleans seminarian Christopher Nalty,
and pulled me aside in the corridor to say with some urgency, "Dahlin', we need to talk." I asked if ten o'clock in her office the next
morning would be convenient and she agreed.

I had been advised that a still-irate Hillary Clinton had planted a
mole in the U.S. embassy to the Holy See, in the person of a young
woman previously employed in the East Wing and now deployed to
the Eternal City as Ambassador Boggs' "assistant". When I arrived
at the embassy, then nestled in a stand of trees on the Aventine Hill
overlooking the Circus Maximus, the mole met me at the door and
with a singular lack of grace led me upstairs to the ambassador's office.
It was obvious that I wasn't going to be able to have the conversation
both Lindy and I wanted with a Clintonista in the room taking notes.
So after the ambassador and I had greeted each other with a hug and
a chaste peck on the cheek, and not wanting Linda to have to play the
heavy, I turned to the mole and said, "Ambassador Boggs and I are
old friends. Do you mind if we speak privately?" Steam metaphori-
cally escaping her ears, the mole left.

"Thank you, dahlin'," said the always-gracious ambassador, who
then got down to business by asking me, with that elegant New

Orleans intonation, "So what's happenin' here?" I replied that I would give her the lowdown with, "As LBJ would have said to your late husband, 'the bark off'." The U.S.-Vatican relationship was a train wreck, thanks to the beatdown that the administration had taken at the Cairo and Beijing conferences, which was due in no small part to adroit Vatican diplomacy. Moreover, there was never going to be agreement on the culture-war issues the Clintons were determined to press in international forums, and the Vatican was just as determined to resist. What to do? Find three issues that the U.S. government and the Holy See could agree on, and work on those for the next three years. As for the rest, I said, "You'll charm the socks off all of them and things will get better because of that."

Lindy, perhaps seeing a glimmer of light in what had hitherto seemed a very dark tunnel (its gloom broken only by the thought of Mass and all those parties), immediately agreed, and we identified three issues where there might be significant common ground: international religious freedom; combating the sex trafficking of women and young girls; and the social impacts of science and technology. Three years later, thanks to some hard and effective work by the octogenarian ambassador and the steady deployment of her exceptional charm, the U.S.-Vatican relationship was back on track, and the groundwork had been laid that would sustain that relationship in the dark days ahead—the days following 9/11.

So assuming that Cokie's brilliant response had some impact on reversing her mother's initial inclination to decline the Vatican embassy, the commentator really did have effect on the things on which commentators comment.

A bit of snark marred the *Washington Post*'s lengthy obituary on Cokie Roberts, to the effect that Cokie didn't just reflect conventional wisdom; she *was* the conventional wisdom. There was an element of truth in that, for all that the sniper in question, a media critic for *Slate*, doubtless wished that he and his comrades were the conventional wisdom. Still, for whatever truth it may have contained, that little bit of postmortem smackdown missed something important about Mary Martha Corinne Morrison Claiborne Boggs Roberts.

On some occasion or other, Cokie and I had fallen into conversation about the controversy du jour and I mentioned Henry Hyde, then the undisputed leader of the pro-life forces in Congress, for whom I was doing some work. To which Cokie responded, "Henry Hyde is the smartest man in Congress. And he's the best debater in the House." *That* was certainly not the conventional wisdom. And it's hard to imagine one of Cokie's fellow NPR-founding mothers (Nina Totenberg, for example) saying any such thing. The compliment bespoke a willingness to think outside the box, at least occasionally; to admire talent and commitment for what they were; and to concede that there might be something other than wickedness, stupidity, and misogyny on the other side of the aisle. It was a virtue that I imagine Cokie learned from her parents, who were far more interested in getting things done in Congress than in making headlines.

I like to think of Cokie and Lindy now reunited, beyond the reach of politics and snark, in a place-beyond-places where a great party is always underway. *Requiescant in pace.*

The Well-Dressed Astronomer
Tycho Brahe (1546–1601)

Among those I'm looking forward to meeting postmortem is Tycho Brahe, one of the first of the great astronomers whose work changed humanity's vision of the cosmos and our place in it. And for one reason in particular: it is said that Tycho never went into his observatory to study the heavens without first putting on his court robes.

Therein lies a lesson.

I was reminded of Tycho's reverence toward the cosmos by the Pioneer 11 mission to Saturn in 1979. In the years of the Carter doldrums, Pioneer's pictures of the ringed planet and the Voyager mission photos of Jupiter were some of the very best good news to reach America, albeit from very far away. They were a reminder of the infinite majesty and splendor of creation, something that Tycho Brahe understood as he put on his palace finery when entering the observatory. Tycho's gesture was no mere aristocratic fetish; it was an act of faith, expressing gratitude for the wonders he was going to study.

This is a profoundly religious attitude. The historian of religions Rudolf Otto wrote more than a century ago that the object of religious faith was the *mysterium tremendum et fascinans* (I leave you to your own translation). Faith, says Otto, begins in awe and wonder. Religious experience means, at least in part, being captured by the sheer wonderfulness of reality and its awesome scope. Seeing those Pioneer 11 pictures from Saturn—and especially those revealing its hitherto unknown sixth ring, which proved that creation is still full of surprises, even for folks raised on instant replay—was a kind of religious experience for many, including me. I hope it also was for at least a few of the scientists at NASA's Ames Research Center in Pasadena.

Another impressive thing about Tycho Brahe was his sense of the terrific excess of creation. It's an attitude we'd all do well to ponder.

Most of us are cheap about creation—not in the sense of thrift and stewardship, but in our myopia about its parade of wonders. How much of the grandeur that's been set before us ever enters our minds and hearts? But unless it does, we're apt not to have much sense of the madly extravagant love of the Father and Creator who put it all there for our delight. It's like the Englishwoman said when questioned about all the money being spent on Queen Elizabeth II's coronation in 1953: "What people like is the sheer excess of it. We lead niggling enough lives these days. Something a bit lavish is good for the soul."

Lavishness that's good for the soul doesn't begin and end with planets and coronations, of course. Anglican theologian-cook Robert Farrar Capon began his delightful book *The Supper of the Lamb* with a meditation on cutting an onion:

> Spending an hour in the society of an onion may be something you have never done before. You feel, perhaps, a certain resistance to the project. Please don't.... Onions are excellent company....
>
> You will note, to begin with, that the onion is a thing, a being, just as you are. Savor that for a moment. This is a Session, a meeting, a society of things. You have, you see, already discovered something: the uniqueness, the placiness of places derives not from abstractions like location, but from confrontations like man-onion.... What really matters is not where we are, but who—what real beings—are with us. In that sense heaven, where we see God face to face through the risen flesh of Jesus, may well be the placiest of all places, as it is the most gloriously material of all meetings.
>
> Beneath this onion's gorgeous paradigm of unnecessary being lies the Act by which it exists.... Hopefully, you will never again argue that the solidities of the world are mere matters of accident, creatures of air and darkness, temporary and meaningless shapes out of nothing. Perhaps you have now seen at least dimly that the uniquenesses of creation are the result of continuous creative support, of effective regard by no mean lover.... He likes onions, therefore they are. The fit, the colors, the smell, the tastes, the textures, the shapes are a response, not to some forgotten decree that there may as well be onions as turnips, but to His present delight—His intimate and immediate joy in all you have seen, and in the thousand other wonders you do not even suspect. With Peter, the onion says, Lord, it is good for us to be here. Yes, says God. *Tov*. Very good.

The Psalmist prays, "Let everything that breathes praise the LORD!" (150:6). For sure. But let's not forget the onions and the planets. They may not breathe, but they praise aplenty. Would that we could praise so well.

The Courtly Shipbuilder
Robert J. Breskovich (1926–1993)

The Pacific Northwest lost one of its noblest sons when Robert John Breskovich died, far too young, on September 4, 1993. Those of us who cherished him also lost the terrestrial company of a singular personality: a man for all seasons, but especially fitted for this one; a splendid companion and generous benefactor; a courtly gentleman of thoughtfulness, panache, and class.

Bob Breskovich was the living refutation of the lie that preconciliar American Catholicism was a benighted ghetto, one in which it was impossible to cultivate spiritual, intellectual, or commercial excellence, much less good taste. No one was more truly an "ethnic Catholic" than Bob Breskovich—and no one better confounded, by the quality of his life, the stereotypes by which Catholics of the old school were (and are) dismissed as so many Neanderthals.

For there were few men along the Puget Sound littoral who were interested in more things; who read more widely; who traveled more extensively; who nurtured a wider company of friends; or who supported a more diverse range of charities. Moreover, Bob Breskovich, whose energies left younger acquaintances exhausted, did everything else he did while running several successful businesses, raising a wonderful family, and, withal, having a lot of fun.

Given the regnant taxonomies, Bob Breskovich was thought to be a conservative, and in many respects he was just that. He believed the past had things to teach the present. He honored the heritage of Western civilization. He declined to believe that modernity had rendered disposable the wisdom of Augustine and Aquinas. He despised political correctness and was chagrined that the Democratic Party he once championed had deteriorated into the party of lifestyle libertinism.

But Bob Breskovich was neither a stick-in-the-mud nor a reactionary. He was, rather, a Burkean figure: a man of generous and liberal sensibility who loved freedom, but who also believed that traditional institutions—family, neighborhood, Church—were the real building blocks of civilization.

Bob Breskovich did not mindlessly resist change. But he wanted social and political change that supported genuine human flourishing, not change that turned men and women into welfare serfs or slaves to their passions. And he wanted ecclesiastical change that broadened our love for the inexhaustible riches of the Christian tradition, not change that reduced the Church to Catholic Lite.

And, just to ensure that his Slavic disputatiousness got a workout from time to time, Bob Breskovich (who knew all about the authoritarian temptation that had crept into the heart of liberalism, political and ecclesiastic) did not hesitate to puncture the pretensions of those who, in the name of openness, were rigidly enforcing new orthodoxies.

He had remarkably little vanity for a man of great accomplishment, but he took a quiet (and wholly justifiable) pride in the things he did; and he did things small and large with equal zest. How proud he was of the handsome inlay with which he enhanced the cabinetry of a crab boat one of his companies had built; it wasn't necessary, but it made for a more beautiful vessel. And, on a far larger canvas, there was the satisfaction he took in building a new business that created jobs for hundreds of people.

Bob Breskovich's people came from the tragic lands of southeastern Europe, where optimism is a luxury that few can afford. From them, and in his own right, he knew suffering from the inside. It taught him an admirable patience that one saw in a striking variety of circumstances—as when he explained the fishing business to a neophyte like me, or the importance of chastity to teenagers. But he was fundamentally a happy man; and his happiness was rooted in a rock-solid faith that the gates of hell would not, after all, prevail.

I loved Bob Breskovich, and at his death I was saddened by the thought that I shall never again, this side of the New Jerusalem, raise a glass, or shoot the breeze, or laugh, or work together with him. But I expect that he is up to his celestial eyeballs in an even grander conversation than he enjoyed here on earth. And I pray that we who loved him here will, someday, and in the mercy of God, be reunited with him there.

Death with Real Dignity
Don J. Briel (1947–2018)

Talk of "death with dignity" in postmodern America tends to be another dreary expression of the Culture of Me: I, the imperial autonomous Self, get to decide when, and how, I die; and the state, by legalizing euthanasia or physician-assisted suicide, has a duty to facilitate my "right to die". The sad emptiness of those claims—and the contrasting deep truths about the human dignity of our suffering and dying—were on display during the last weeks of the consequential life of Don Briel, who died far too early.

His was not a household name, but Don Briel was one of the most important and effective Catholic educators of the post–Vatican II era. As too many Catholic colleges and universities careened into the incoherence that marks so many of their secular counterparts, Briel set about creating "Catholic Studies" programs that would restore Catholic intellectual, cultural, liturgical, and lifestyle identity to institutions of higher learning that bore the name "Catholic"—but often didn't seem to know what that meant. Don Briel did know, however.

"Catholic" meant a deep dive into the riches of the liberal arts, including philosophy and theology. "Catholic" meant an experience of living in an intentional Catholic community defined by rhythms of prayer, liturgical worship, and service as well as study. "Catholic" meant an immersion in the Church's aesthetic heritage in art, architecture, and music. And "Catholic" meant spiritual direction in aid of vocational discernment.

The model Catholic Studies program that Briel created at the University of St. Thomas in St. Paul, Minnesota, included a year on the program's Rome campus. And to visit, teach, dine, and pray at that campus was to get a glimpse into what Don Briel's intellectual and spiritual hero, Saint John Henry Newman, meant by "the idea of a university": a community of conversation resting on the convictions that there is truth, and that truth sets us free in the deepest meaning of human liberation. Newman never managed to pull it off in Ireland; Don Briel came very close, in far different circumstances, in the program he created on the bluffs above the Mississippi and at the University of St. Thomas' satellite on the banks of the Tiber.

In late 2017, Don and I were catching up by phone after Christmas when he told me that some blood work he'd had done recently had revealed leukemia. That was a blow, obviously, but the hammer really fell a short time later, when, after pondering various treatment options, he was informed that further tests had revealed his to be one of perhaps a hundred cases in recorded medical history of two simultaneous forms of acute leukemia. Which meant that no treatment was possible. None. He had, at best, a month to live.

We had talked about almost everything over the twenty-plus years of our friendship: books; art; the follies of politics, political and ecclesiastical; educational reform; our families and their triumphs and struggles. But the conversations I had with Don while the clock was literally running out are the ones I shall cherish in memory forever. He was completely calm and cheerful, and lucid until very near the end. And he accepted as a great gift both the fact and the manner of his dying—at home, nursed by the sisters of a religious community that had grown out of his work, and ministered to by priests he had helped train. Shortly after he had received the evil decree, we spent one forty-minute conversation discussing what novels he might read (I suggested Waugh's *Helena*) and what single malts he should try (the answer turned out to be Lagavulin) as he passed from this life into eternity. Another conversation involved his beloved Newman, and Don remarked, with his usual insight and sense of irony, on how various personalities in the Church of 2018—now, located on the port side of the Barque of Peter—were making the extravagant, ultramontanist claims for Pope Francis that the Catholic reactionaries of the mid-nineteenth century had once made for Pope Pius IX.

We discussed whether, in the Kingdom, one had to wait in line to talk with certain great personalities of the past, as Don would certainly want to get acquainted with Newman and his other intellectual mentor, historian Christopher Dawson. During that conversation, I told him a story about the famous biblical scholar Father Raymond Brown, a passionate defender of the historical-critical method of biblical exegesis, who was once asked whether he was looking forward to meeting Saint John (on whom he had written extensively) in heaven. "Yes," Father Brown admitted, he was; but he was worried about one thing. "What's that, Ray?", someone asked. "I'm worried," Father Brown replied, that when "I ask Saint John, 'Why did you write that there were "a hundred and fifty-three large fish [on the seashore where the disciples met the risen Jesus, in John 21]"?', Saint John is going to reply, 'Because there were a hundred and fifty-three of them.'" Don and I laughed, not least in an appreciation of a great scholar who had the grace to laugh at his own exegetical method. And we remarked, with a certain sadness, on how little there was of that gentlemanly graciousness among certain Catholic intellectuals of the progressive persuasion today.

Friends who came to visit him during his last weeks—and they came from all over the United States and Europe—met a man living the supreme moment of his life: the moment in which he would make the final commitment of his life back to the God who had given it to him, with grace, and faith, and true dignity. He did not complain. Rather, he said time and again how wonderful it was to be able to be with his children and grandchildren, and with so many old friends, all at once. It was an experience of the communion of saints, here and now—and an anticipation of the communion of saints in its fullness at the Throne of Grace, contemplating the Eternal Triune Love that, as Dante wrote, "moves the sun and all the stars".

February 15, 2018, the day of Don Briel's death, happened to be the Thursday after Ash Wednesday; and in the Lenten station-church pilgrimage in Rome, in which Don had often participated, that Thursday's station is the Basilica of San Giorgio in Velabro—John Henry Newman's titular pastorate in Rome after he was named a cardinal by Pope Leo XIII. It was an entirely fitting day for Don Briel to die, and as his son Matt held the phone to his ear so that I could speak to him the day before, I told him that I was sure that Newman was waiting to welcome him to the fellowship of the blessed.

Newman had had inscribed on the cross over his grave, *Ex umbris et imaginibus in veritatem*—"From shadows and phantasms into the truth." That is what Don Briel did for thousands of students: he led them from the shadowlands of late-modern decadence and postmodern incoherence into the truths that reflect the Truth who is the

Triune God. Newman would have appreciated that, I said to my friend, and would want to offer a helping hand at Don's Passover.

So as his family and friends bade farewell, in this life, to a great teacher and a great soul, we remembered John Henry Newman's prayer and offered it for the late, great Don Briel:

> May He support us all the day long, 'til the shades lengthen and the evening comes, and the busy world is hushed, and the fever of life is over, and our work is done. Then in His mercy may He give us a safe lodging, and a holy rest, and peace at last.

The Publicist

William F. Buckley, Jr. (1925–2008)

Who were the most publicly influential American Catholics of the twentieth century?

By shaping Vatican II's teaching on Church and state, Father John Courtney Murray, S.J., helped turn Catholicism into the world's foremost institutional advocate of religious freedom. John F. Kennedy put Catholics into play at the highest level of our national politics. Fulton J. Sheen gave Catholicism an engaging public face on radio and television for years. Thomas Merton's books have sold in the millions. Henry Hyde was the congressional paladin of the pro-life movement and its most significant legislator. Antonin Scalia reconfigured American jurisprudence from the Supreme Court.

If by "publicly influential", however, we mean a Catholic whose ideas changed the way Americans think, who reshaped our politics and our public policy, and whose influence seems likely to endure, then William F. Buckley, Jr., who died on February 27, 2008, must be given his due.

The most telling thing about Bill Buckley, the man, is that so many people thought of him as a friend. Underneath those faux High Anglican tones and that disheveled, preppie look was a genuine democrat (if his shade will pardon the term): a man who treated junior staffers and unheard-of authors with an openness and cordiality rarely found in world-famous figures. He was "Bill" the first time you met him, and "Bill" he remained.

There was a lot of little boy—and a lot of rebel—in him; both traits help account for his infectious enthusiasm, his joie de vivre, and his democratic personal instincts. Above all—or, perhaps better, beneath it all—Bill Buckley was a Catholic gentleman whose faith had taught him how to treat others, including those with whom he disagreed.

The obituaries published at his death stressed his remarkable productivity as author, editor, columnist, lecturer, and television personality, to which he added the skills of an accomplished musician
and sailor. He was not without ego, but he could turn his humor on
himself. Running for mayor of New York, he was asked what he
would do if elected: "Demand a recount" was the immediate riposte.

His first book, *God and Man at Yale*, was excoriated by the American educational establishment of 1951 as the reactionary ramblings of
an intellectual pup who hadn't been housebroken. In the twenty-first
century, *GAMAY* (as Bill referred to it) stands as an eerily prescient
preview of the intellectual and moral implosion that's taken place
in elite American higher education over the past half-century. His
best novel, *Stained Glass*, was a penetrating exploration of the moral
dilemmas of statecraft.

He was not politically infallible, and he probably shared Barry
Goldwater's regret at having criticized, on constitutional grounds,
federally mandated desegregation. No one who ever knew the
man could imagine him a bigot, however. And his tolerant civility
extended far beyond the sphere of his personal relationships. Analysts
credit Buckley with creating the "fusion" conservatism that, via the
magazine he founded, *National Review*, brought the social/cultural
conservatives, the pro-market conservatives, and the anticommunist/
national security conservatives into one politically potent tent, thus
making possible the Reagan Revolution. Which is true enough.
But Bill's even greater public service was to purge the conservative
movement of the anti-Semitism, racism, xenophobia, and isolationism that had infested the fever swamps of the American Right in
the FDR period and beyond. There was no room for bigotry in Bill
Buckley's big tent.

In 1949, Lionel Trilling, the Columbia literary critic who embodied the pragmatic, results-oriented liberalism of Franklin Roosevelt
and Harry Truman, deplored those American conservatives who do
not "express themselves in ideas but only in action or in irritable mental gestures which seek to resemble ideas". Bill Buckley changed all
that, by his own intellectual efforts and sparkling personality, as well
as by nurturing the thought, the writing, and the careers of countless
others. If, as President Barack Obama conceded in one of his more
candid moments, the conservative world was for years the center of

ideas in American politics, a lot of the credit for creating a true intellectual marketplace in our public life must go to Bill Buckley.

He once told his son, Christopher, that the active life was an antidote to melancholy. Now beyond the reach of melancholia, may he rest in peace.

Enemy Become Friend
Charles W. Colson (1931–2012)

Back in the days when Chuck Colson was willing to run over his grandmother for Richard Nixon, I would have happily done the same to Mr. Colson. Well, that was then. And now I have to say, reflecting on twenty years of friendship and collaboration with Chuck Colson, that I never met a more thoroughly converted Christian, a more ecumenically serious Christian, or a more tenacious Christian. He was a man whom I came, not just to respect, but to love.

Our lives began to intersect in the early 1990s, when Herbert Schlossberg, the evangelical author, buttonholed me at a Washington reception and expressed concern about the ongoing fracture between Catholics and evangelical Protestants, two communities that Herb thought should be working together to shore up America's public moral culture. I mentioned Herb's concern to Richard John Neuhaus; Neuhaus called Colson; and within a matter of months "Evangelicals and Catholics Together" was born.

What began as co-belligerency in the American culture war soon evolved in ways none of us had anticipated. Led by Neuhaus and Colson, and prodded by such towering intellects as Avery Dulles, S.J., and J.I. Packer, ECT, as we called it, developed into what was arguably the most important theological encounter ever between evangelical Protestants and Catholics. Issues we had once imagined to be completely off-the-table—Mary, the communion of saints, justification—were not only broached but examined, pondered, and prayed over. And the result was not only a deepening of fellowship but a refinement of thought. That a leading evangelical theologian should write a book on Mary-for-evangelicals says something about the miles traveled, and the centuries of misunderstanding bridged, in those conversations.

ECT returned to the culture wars in 2010, this time in defense of religious freedom. And just before Chuck Colson died, the U.S.

bishops' Ad Hoc Committee for Religious Liberty commended and cited the ECT statement, "In Defense of Religious Freedom", that Chuck had helped push to completion.

Life with Chuck Colson also involved adventures. My favorite took place in Rome, early in the new century. Just before the opening of a conference held in the old Synod Hall of the Apostolic Palace, I ran into Colson, who asked if I might do him a favor. Obviously, I replied. Well, Chuck said, he had met John Paul II on several occasions, but his wife, Patty, a Catholic, had never met the Pope and would be ecstatic if that could be arranged. Nothing easier, I said—at which point Chuck asked if he could bring along another Major Evangelical Figure (as I shall discretely style him) and his wife. No problem, said I.

So Patty Colson, Chuck, Major Evangelical Figure, and Mrs. Major Evangelical Figure met John Paul II, and Chuck called me the night of the general audience to express his thanks. I then asked if he thought a picture of the encounter in the English edition of the Vatican newspaper, L'Osservatore Romano, would serve our common ecumenical purposes. Chuck, initially enthusiastic, then got cautious: "Wait; I'd better check with [Major Evangelical Figure]." The next day I got another phone call from Chuck: "Don't do anything. The Pope was sitting when he received us, and [Major Evangelical Figure]'s picture was taken when he was down on one knee in front of the Pope. He's afraid his fundraising will collapse if that picture gets out." I laughed, assured him that I would abandon any idea of having the photo run in the Vatican newspaper—and reflected on the still-supple political instincts of a man who found his true vocation only after being driven out of politics by Watergate.

Chuck knew the threat that Major Evangelical Figure feared: at the beginning of our common work, Colson's leadership in ECT cost Prison Fellowship, the marvelous ministry he founded, millions of dollars in lost donations. Chuck took the hit and soldiered on because he believed that the truth of Christ would eventually prevail over hardened hearts. It was a conviction he had come to from hard personal experience, both his own and that of the convicts with whom he worked. And it made him one of the great Christian witnesses of our time.

The Trade Unionist

William C. Doherty, Jr. (1926–2011)

In December 1980, I spent several hours talking with Mike Hammer, a field representative in El Salvador of the American Institute for Free Labor Development (AIFLD). As an overseas development affiliate of the AFL-CIO, AIFLD was trying to bring some sense to the polarized politics of El Salvador, a country coming apart at the seams. A few weeks after we met, that violent polarization cost Mike Hammer his life.

When Hammer and two of his AIFLD colleagues were murdered in El Salvador in January 1981, I wrote a memorial essay in the Seattle *Weekly*, praising these martyrs for decency and democracy. Such were the politics of the time that this tribute to three good men got me into the hottest of hot water with the Seattle-area Left, represented by the Committee in Solidarity with the People of El Salvador, referred to in common parlance by its initials, CISPES. (Thirty years later, when the Mitrokhin Archive, a huge cache of KGB documents, was published, it was revealed that CISPES was a front created by the KGB, the Soviet secret intelligence service, to advance communist interests in Latin America.) The memory of those debates is not what I cherish, however, in thinking back on this episode. What I remember is that my memorial essay was reprinted in AIFLD's newsletter and became the occasion for my meeting AIFLD's longtime leader, William Charles Doherty, Jr., who died on August 28, 2011.

Bill Doherty was one of the great Catholic laymen of twentieth-century America. A bear of a man who had been a defensive lineman at Catholic University during his student days, Bill dedicated his professional life to trade unionism as an instrument of democracy-building (and hence peace-making) in Latin America. Free trade unions, he believed, were crucial components of the civil society that made democracy possible. By helping build those kinds of worker associations, Bill and his AIFLD colleagues were not only giving the poor the tools by which to pull themselves and their families out of poverty; they were giving democracy a chance in places where it had never taken root.

When I brought Bill Doherty to Seattle to speak, some of the salient aspects of his singular personality quickly became evident. The first question he asked me, on arrival, was, "Where can I go to Mass tomorrow morning?" A daily communicant, Bill prepared for political combat by prayer and the sacraments, his deep faith nourished intellectually by his fidelity to Catholic social doctrine. Then there was his contempt for the juvenile Leftism of CISPES and its fellow travelers, on whom he heaped scorn and ridicule with relish. Having fought communists for the control of trade unions throughout the Western Hemisphere, Bill Doherty wasn't about to take any guff from the pre-grunge, pre-Starbucks radicals of the Puget Sound area. They tried to call him a tool of the propertied class. "How dare you call me an oligarch?" he roared back.

Bill Doherty was an equal opportunity opponent of tyranny, whether it was the communist tyranny threatening El Salvador and Nicaragua or the Rightist tyranny entrenched in Chile, Argentina, and Paraguay. He fought them all and he enjoyed the battle. He never hated markets; he wanted them to work fairly, for everyone. He didn't believe in class warfare; he believed in building the infrastructure of freedom. He cheered John Paul II's assault on communism in Central and Eastern Europe, just as he worked to help give organizational expression to the democratic revolution that John Paul encouraged in Augusto Pinochet's Chile.

Like others of his generation of lay Catholic leaders, Bill Doherty was a political liberal who believed in the widest possible participation in government, an economic pragmatist who wanted to open networks of productivity and exchange to everyone, and a Christian radical who believed that the Gospel was the truth of the world. The stupidities (and worse) of many Catholic activists' and journalists' approach to Central America in the 1980s grieved him. But he never lost faith, and he was always willing to welcome converts to the pro-democracy movement. He was a big man in every sense of the word; the biggest thing about him was his big heart.

He now lives in the embrace of the divine solidarity.

The Overseas Brit and Sichuan Country Girl
Audrey Donnithorne (1922–2020)

The first two sentences of Audrey Donnithorne's autobiography, *China in Life's Foreground*, suggest something of her character, independence of mind, and dry sense of humor: "I am an Overseas Brit and a Sichuan country girl. My grandparents were born on three different continents, but all were intensely British, especially, perhaps, the duskier among them."

Born on November 27, 1922, at a Quaker mission hospital in rural China, the self-styled "Sichuan country girl" died in Hong Kong on June 8, 2020. In ninety-seven and a half years of an extraordinary life, Audrey Donnithorne navigated a kaleidoscope of experiences that rank her as one of the most remarkable Catholics of modern times and a genuine heroine of the faith.

Her Anglican missionary parents traced their evangelicalism to the Clapham Sect social reformers and the great William Wilberforce. Kidnapped by bandits as a two-and-a-half-year-old child and held captive for weeks with her parents, she experienced the brutal Japanese war in China as a teenager and lived for a time in Chiang Kai-shek's ramshackle capital, Chongqing (known in those days as Chungking). She left China for wartime Great Britain via a dangerous flight over "the Hump" (the Himalayas), followed by a slow, tedious voyage around the Cape of Good Hope and through the U-boat-infested waters of the Atlantic. While working in military intelligence at the British War Office, she survived the German V-1 buzz bomb attacks on London and converted to Catholicism. During her studies in economics at Oxford after the war, she heard Monsignor Ronald Knox preach at the university's Catholic chaplaincy and befriended a chemistry student named Margaret Roberts, better known in later life as Margaret Thatcher. Frustrated with the abstractions of economic theorists, she never took a doctorate; yet her 1967 book, *China's Economic System*, remains a definitive work on Maoist

economics and continues to draw the respect of serious China scholars. While conducting a seminar at Hebrew University, she found
herself in Jerusalem during the Yom Kippur War. Earlier, she had
tasted Mao Zedong's Great Cultural Revolution in Hong Kong
and Macau, and her robust wit was evident in her recollection of
one Cultural Revolution absurdity: the revolutionary slogan "Down
with Running Dogs", displayed right next to the Macau Canidrome,
the only racetrack for greyhounds in Asia. (In her autobiography, she
also noted that another bit of adolescent rhetoric painted on a church,
"Down with the Blessed Mother of God", was "one of the strangest
fulfillments of [Mary's] prophecy that 'all generations shall call me
blessed'".) She taught at Canberra's Australian National University
for years, and after her retirement from the classroom Down Under
she was affiliated with the Center of Asian Studies at the University
of Hong Kong.

Audrey Donnithorne was always where things were happening.
But whatever the surface similarities between her amazing *curriculum
vitae* and *Zelig* or *Forrest Gump*, Audrey was not fiction and Audrey
was not accidental. Her life was providential. And the story of her
life is the story of a woman of valor, cooperating with divine grace
to be what she believed herself vocationally called to be: doing what
she could to improve the lives of others. A world-class scholar with
a talent for languages and connections, she was also the model of a
New Evangelization Catholic long before the term "New Evangelization" became part of the global Catholic vocabulary.

Before being banned from there by the authorities, dubious of
her connections, she traveled frequently to mainland China from her
Hong Kong home, always looking for ways to help the struggling
Chinese Church. A strong advocate of religious freedom for all, she
knew that this first of civil rights was essential to a just society.
She helped fund the rebuilding or building of churches and the
education of seminarians. She worked with Caritas Hong Kong to
help post–Cultural Revolution Chinese Catholics start small businesses that could be part of a financial support system for desperately
poor parishes. In her Hong Kong apartment, she and her friends
packed up books, missals, breviaries, Bibles, and other religious
materials and then dispatched these Catholic CARE packages into
the ironically named People's Republic of China: food for the souls

of the Chinese people she loved with a clear-eyed view of their complex humanity.

Perhaps most importantly, she worked to build bridges of understanding and cooperation between what are often, and simplistically, thought to be China's deeply and permanently divided "underground Catholics" and "patriotic Catholics". Knowing the vast differences within China and understanding Chinese culture from the inside, she knew that things are rarely simple or straightforward in the Middle Kingdom. A very practical person, Audrey Donnithorne took situations and personalities one at a time, never trying to force people or circumstances onto some Procrustean bed of theory or ideology. That approach made a real difference. Her hard, patient, and effective work helped bring illicitly ordained Chinese bishops into full communion with the Bishop of Rome during the pontificate of John Paul II—work for which she was awarded the Papal Cross *Pro Ecclesia et Pontifice*.

At the same time, she understood that the Chinese leadership under Xi Jinping was bent on creating a "Sino-Catholicism" for its own purposes. And it is scandalous that those responsible for China in the Vatican in the second decade of the twenty-first century seem never to have taken counsel with Audrey Donnithorne, who knew far more about China than any Italian papal diplomat. Perhaps her longstanding collaboration with the redoubtable Cardinal Joseph Zen, S.D.B., bishop emeritus of Hong Kong, branded her a "nonfriend" in certain Roman circles. If so, the losers from that sorry misperception were the architects of today's Vatican China policy, an ongoing disaster for the Church's evangelical mission on the mainland.

Toward the end of her 2019 autobiography, which is largely *allegro* and *dolce*, she nonetheless penned a sharp-edged reflection on the Holy See's approach to China today that is worth pondering:

> I often wish that the monsignori in the [Vatican] Secretariat of State, instead of spending time and effort on trying to re-establish diplomatic links with the Chinese government, would go out on the streets of Rome and look for any Chinese tourists who seem bewildered and offer to show them around the sights. On one of my last visits to Rome, in the 1990s, I noticed two young Chinese near St. Peter's, looking puzzled and consulting their guidebook. I went up to them and, after their surprise that I addressed them in Chinese, asked if they

would like to be shown around the basilica; they gladly agreed.... Let us remember that on the birthday of the Church, when the Holy Spirit descended on that prayerful gathering of believers, their immediate reaction was not to discuss how to deal with Caesar in the imperial capital, but to go out into the streets around them to speak both to the locals and to the visitors from overseas who were thronging the city.

Audrey and I never met in person but, via email and telephone, we became friends and colleagues because of John Paul II.

Although there are, as of 2020, fourteen language editions of *Witness to Hope*, the first volume of my John Paul II biography, the only translations that the Pope really urged me to get done were German and Chinese. With strong support from Cardinals Joseph Ratzinger and Joachim Meisner, a German translation and edition were arranged without too much difficulty. Chinese was a different matter. It was obvious that the book could not be produced in the People's Republic. A Chinese edition of *Witness to Hope* published in Taiwan would never make it into mainland China, and the whole point of the exercise was for John Paul to be able to "visit" China through the book. So the only serious option was translation and publication in Hong Kong.

Cardinal Zen's predecessor as bishop of Hong Kong was a rather timid man, whose response to my inquiries was that such a project would be terribly expensive, not commercially viable, and likely inopportune—this, despite the fact that the Pope himself had urged the book's translation and publication in Chinese. Such reticence disappeared when Joseph Zen became bishop. In the meantime, as I was trying to get done what the Pope wanted done, I "met" Audrey Donnithorne through the good offices of Grace Goodell of the Johns Hopkins University School of Advanced International Studies and we quickly became email correspondents. I explained the situation, and in her typical, pragmatic way, Audrey took the problem in hand and, with Cardinal Zen, solved it. Funds were found for a translation; a translator was engaged; and at our last dinner on December 15, 2004, I was able to tell John Paul II that a Chinese edition of *Witness to Hope* would in fact happen.

It took a while, not least because of the challenge of accurately translating a thousand-page book into a character-based language so that my meaning (and, more importantly, John Paul's) was precisely conveyed. A week or so before she died, Audrey sent me a brief video, thanking me for my friendship and prayers and apologizing for not having done more to get the Chinese *Witness to Hope* project completed. That was, of course, not her fault; but it was entirely in character for her to imagine that it was, and that she had somehow failed me. So it was another happy, providential coincidence that, a few days later, Cardinal Zen wrote me with the news that the translation had finally been finished and the presses were ready to run with the long-gestated Chinese edition of *Witness to Hope*. With the kind assistance of two of Audrey's longtime friends, William McGurn of the *Wall Street Journal* and Teresa Lai, wife of the intrepid Hong Kong democracy activist and philanthropist Jimmy Lai, I was able to get word of this to Audrey shortly before her death.

Audrey Donnithorne died with Teresa Lai and the Lais' daughter Claire praying the Rosary with her. Her ashes are buried in her native Sichuan, at the Church of Our Lady of Lourdes. In the future, after the current Chinese regime and its assault on religious freedom is a bad memory, that church should become a place of pilgrimage. Audrey would scoff at the notion, I'm sure. But she was a true confessor of the faith and, in God's providence, I trust that she will be long remembered as such.

Leader of "The Few"
Hugh Dowding (1882–1970)

On Sunday, September 15, 1940, Winston Churchill and his wife, Clementine, were driven from the prime minister's official country estate, Chequers, to the nearby village of Uxbridge and a Royal Air Force station, the headquarters from which Air Vice-Marshal Keith Park was directing the RAF's No. 11 Group against the onslaught of the German Luftwaffe in Southern England. When the prime minister and his wife walked into No. 11 Group's Operations Room, Park, a doughty New Zealander who flew his own personal Hurricane fighter, said, "I don't know whether anything will happen today. At present, all is quiet."

That soon changed. As Churchill looked down from the balcony, young women began moving markers on a large map table, like croupiers at a casino. The markers indicated Luftwaffe bombers and fighters queuing up over France, then heading to England on what many regard as the decisive day in the Battle of Britain—the outcome of which determined the course of World War II in Europe. As the numbers of approaching German planes grew to 250, Park scrambled sixteen RAF fighter squadrons and called in another five from No. 12 Group, based in the English Midlands.

By noon, No. 11 Group was fully engaged in an aerial brawl over the entire south of England, and some of Park's Spitfires and Hurricanes began returning to their bases to refuel and re-arm. As the German attack continued and Park called in another three squadrons from No. 12 Group, Churchill, who had been uncharacteristically quiet, turned to the air vice-marshal and asked, "What other reserves have we?" The answer was grim: "There are none." As Churchill later wrote in *The Second World War*, "The odds were great; our margins, small; the stakes infinite."

The odds, the margins, and the stakes had been all of that since Hermann Goering had decided in mid-1940 to end Britain's bulldog recalcitrance and bomb the United Kingdom into a negotiated peace. He failed, in part, because of the inferiority of some of his aircraft and the technological breakthroughs made by Britain's "boffins", the scientists who invented radar in the 1930s and who later broke German military codes. But as always in war, the moral was to the material by a large factor and the RAF was replete with heroes. Sadly, their stories are now largely forgotten.

More often than not, the British pilots who flew those Hurricanes and Spitfires were a year or two removed from secondary school—and not just elite schools like Eton and Harrow, for the majority of RAF fighter pilots in the Battle of Britain came from less exalted social circles. These youngsters were joined by Polish and Czech volunteers who found their way to Britain to continue their countries' struggle against the Third Reich. The RAF's young fighter pilots often flew four or five missions a day, in the most physically and mentally taxing circumstances imaginable; fully one-third of them were killed, gravely wounded (often by horrible burns), or captured during the late summer months of 1940. Well might Churchill have said, after the Luftwaffe tacitly conceded defeat, that never in the field of human conflict had so much been owed by so many to so few.

But those brave pilots would not have stood a chance had they not been led by another largely forgotten figure: Air Chief Marshal Sir Hugh Dowding, who conceived the system of radar stations linked to centralized fighter control that made it possible for group leaders like Keith Park to deploy their limited resources in the most effective way possible. And it was Dowding who confronted Churchill in June 1940, as the French were collapsing before the Nazi Blitzkrieg, and made the prime minister face the grim arithmetic of the moment: no more British fighter squadrons could be frittered away in a futile effort to save what was unsalvageable on the other side of the English Channel. Winston Churchill, who had promised the French more RAF planes, was not an easy man to contradict. But Dowding had the courage to do so. And in saving the RAF's fighter squadrons from being chewed to pieces in the Battle of France, which he knew was lost, Dowding made his young pilots' victory in the Battle of Britain possible.

Eight decades after their exploits, these heroes are too often forgotten. That is shameful, for they played an indispensable role in
saving the liberties of the Western world. May they rest in the peace
that they were not granted in this life.

Abraham Lincoln in Full Pontificals
Avery Dulles, S.J. (1918–2008)

It was wonderful to count the late Cardinal Avery Dulles, S.J., as a friend for almost a quarter-century. Truth to tell, though, I had "known" Avery long before I met him; I had begun reading him when two of his books, *Apologetics and the Biblical Christ* and *Models of the Church*, were assigned in my sophomore-year college theology classes, back in the (gasp!) first Nixon administration. When we first met in Washington, somewhere around 1985, Avery's reputation as Catholic America's unique theological reference point was well-established. What was immediately evident about the man himself was his unaffected naturalness, his preternatural calm, and his good humor.

From the mid-1970s on, Avery was a sign of contradiction within an ever more Left-leaning U.S. Catholic theological establishment. He was one of the Catholic signatories of the 1975 "Hartford Appeal for Theological Affirmation", an ecumenical challenge to then-dominant revisionist and secularizing tendencies in academic theology. Dubbed the "Hartford Heresies" by those who rightly considered themselves to be in its crosshairs, the Appeal in fact marked one of the points at which Catholic theology in America began to re-ground itself in the Church's ancient and ongoing tradition, rather than imagining that theology (and everything else, for that matter) had started all over again with the Second Vatican Council.

Taking a leadership role wasn't a particularly pleasant task for Avery, a private man who relished serious argument but had no taste for polemics. Yet he acceded to the wishes of his peers and served as president of the Catholic Theological Society of America during one of its most difficult periods: a CTSA-commissioned study on sexual morality couldn't bring itself to condemn bestiality; Church authorities who hadn't been cowed by the professoriate were (rightly) aghast; the experience of defending orthodoxy while leading the society through the ecclesiastical donnybrook that followed doubtless reinforced Avery's long-standing dislike of the spotlight.

If there is an American aristocracy, Avery Dulles was certainly part of it, but he never made a point of his lineage, though his great-grandfather, his great-uncle, and his father had all served as secretary of state (under Presidents Benjamin Harrison, Woodrow Wilson, and Dwight D. Eisenhower). And as his father's reputation came under fire from historians stewed in the juices of the Sixties, Avery remained a man of deep, if usually understated, filial piety. In a 1994 lecture at Princeton, "John Foster Dulles: His Religious and Philosophical Heritage", Avery met the fashionable liberal critique of Foster Dulles and his alleged marriage of hyper-Calvinism to American chauvinism in the calm, scholarly spirit with which he handled theological controversy. His conclusion was both just and loving: "At a distance of a generation or two, I think we may judge that my father made the kind of contribution to which he felt called—that of a Christian layman concerned with developing a world order consonant with Christ and the Gospel. [Thus] he was able to make a coherent and, to me, convincing case that a nation cannot be enduringly strong and prosperous without adherence to strong spiritual and moral principles."

My favorite Dulles memory, however, involves a black-and-white photo, not a lecture or a book. In it, Avery, his lanky torso clad only in a T-shirt, is standing at the bar of New York's Union League Club, having just performed a modest striptease for an ecumenical and interreligious group of theologians.

It was, in a sense, my fault: in a fit of whimsy, I had had T-shirts made from the cover of my book *Catholicism and the Renewal of American Democracy*, for which Avery had kindly provided a glowing front-cover blurb. One of the shirts went to Father Dulles, with a note explaining that this would make him the best-dressed theologian at Fordham University. Some weeks later, at a meeting organized by Richard John Neuhaus (then still a Lutheran), Avery caused consternation in the Union League Club bar by taking off his suit jacket (itself a grave offense in the very proper ULC) before starting to peel off his shirt. "He's had a stroke," people thought. "Somebody call 911!"

But there was no stroke. Father Dulles just wanted to show off his new T-shirt. The photo of Avery and his crooked grin, surrounded by Catholic, Protestant, and Jewish theologians cracking up, is one I shall cherish *ad multos annos*.

And then there was his cardinalate. As had become customary, Pope John Paul II had announced the names of the men he intended to create cardinals at the noon Sunday Angelus in St. Peter's Square. Richard Neuhaus happened to be in town that day, so my wife, Joan, and I had invited him, along with Michael and Karen Novak, to dinner. We had just sat down at the table after drinking a toast to our friend's red hat when the phone rang in my study.

It was Avery. After absorbing my congratulations, he said, "Yes, well, that's all fine, but look, I don't have to become a bishop, do I?" A bit taken aback, I said, "No, I think you just write the Pope and ask to be dispensed from the canonical requirement of cardinals being bishops; he's done it for others and he'll surely do it for you. But why are you so worried about being a bishop, Avery?" "Because I'm too old to be running around New York doing confirmations," replied John Foster Dulles' son.

The consistory was, to put it mildly, memorable. Avery was last in a line of forty-two new cardinals and knelt before John Paul to receive the red biretta. He then bent over the Pope's hand to kiss the papal ring—and the biretta fell into John Paul's lap. The Pope put it back on Avery's head; Avery bowed again, and the recalcitrant headgear fell into the pontifical lap, again. At which point Avery took the biretta, jammed it onto his head, and the vast crowd in St. Peter's Square gave him a big round of applause.

Later that day, at a reception in the cortile of the Pontifical North American College, Avery asked for a chair in which to sit while receiving the many who wanted to greet him. I watched the scene from a distance and couldn't help thinking how much he looked like one of his intellectual heroes, John Henry Newman, in the portrait painted by Sir John Everett Millais.

John Paul had given Avery the Church of the Holy Names of Jesus and Mary as his title, or Roman pastorate. It was an apt choice, for the church had once been the *titulus* of Saint Robert Bellarmine, a theologian of the Counter-Reformation whom Avery admired. The church, on the Corso, was in the care of the Discalced Augustinians, and when Avery's guests met them prior to the Mass at which he would "take possession" of the church, you could see the dollar signs in their eyes—surely this son of American aristocrats would lavish a bit of his wealth on their church. Little did they know that their new cardinal-titular fixed his shoes with duct tape and gave all his substantial book royalties to his religious order.

But the great moment of that evening came when Avery processed up the central aisle at the beginning of Mass, wearing the miter and pectoral cross and carrying the crozier appropriate to his new rank. We were all a bit shocked to see him like that, but Jody Bottum caught the moment perfectly when he said, in a stage whisper, "Now we know what Abraham Lincoln would have looked like in full pontificals."

Avery's cardinalate did not change his sartorial habits very much. Some months after the consistory, I got a note from Father Joseph Lienhard, a fellow Jesuit and distinguished patristics scholar on the Fordham faculty: "Thanks for the souvenirs of Avery's investiture.... He looks great walking around the campus in a faded blue windbreaker and pectoral cross." Nor did Avery's new eminence change his relentless work habits. The post-polio syndrome that would eventually kill him robbed him of the power of speech, but he could communicate through a keyboard attached to a screen. Shortly before he died, Avery was visited by a fellow theologian, Father Robert Imbelli, who, at the end of their conversation, said, "Avery, is there anything I can do for you?" To which the cardinal replied, tapping out the message on the keyboard, "Put some more paper in the printer."

There was a book review to finish, you see.

A Meaningful Cosmos

Albert Einstein (1879–1955)

Two ikons—one painted in the twelfth century, the other composed in the twentieth—were once side by side in my study. The Vladimir Mother of God, which pious tradition says was brought from Kyiv to Moscow in 1395 to help defend the city from Tamarlane, was the most famous ikon in Russia. Philippe Halsman's 1947 photographic portrait of Albert Einstein was an apt companion piece. Both reflected the human capacity, under God's grace, to pass through tragedy into truth.

Modernity is distinguished by many quasi-heretical ideas, but few have been more damaging than the notion that man is meant only for happiness and personal fulfillment. The idea came, in part, as a necessary corrective to theologies that taught a distorted picture of a corrupt humanity that was to be denied and escaped rather than redeemed and transformed. But in the hands of pop psychologists, talk show gurus, and religious trivializers, the idea that sin is just a matter of bad emotional adjustment has become the perceived wisdom of the age. Personal responsibility has, consequently, been drastically eroded (parents, spouses, siblings, capitalism, and "patriarchy" are all to blame, you know). Yet in the midst of the writhing, few seem to have noticed that we really aren't much happier than our pre-Freudian ancestors.

I don't mean to suggest that God created us for misery. I do mean to suggest that, when you look into the sad, wise eyes of the Vladimir Mother of God or of Halsman's Einstein, you learn that duty, obligation, loyalty, and painstaking work are as revelatory of the meaning of human life as pleasure, ecstasy, or "doing your own thing".

Pondering the human mystery of tragedy transformed into grace, one bumps right up against the fact that irony is one of history's recurring patterns. Einstein was a perfect example: the lifelong pacifist whose letter to President Roosevelt helped launch the Manhattan

Project and the atomic bombings of Hiroshima and Nagasaki; the Zionist who put peace with the Arabs at the top of the agenda, but who finally agreed that it was necessary to fight; the physicist who radically changed our understanding of the cosmos, only to be read out of the scholarly mainstream and its consensus on "indeterminacy" because of an essentially theological intuition that "God doesn't play dice with the universe."

Sustaining faith in the elemental meaningfulness of creation (which is faith in the fundamental graciousness of the Creator) isn't always easy, now or ever. Living through the ironies and the contradictions involves two important dimensions of spiritual courage: the intrepidity of intuition and the virtue of curiosity. Einstein exemplified both.

Einstein broke with his colleagues in physics over the notion, first articulated by Werner Heisenberg, that at the subatomic level of reality the reassuring principles of cause-and-effect that allow precise measurements give way to statistical probabilities. Einstein wouldn't wear it and spent the last part of his career searching for a "unified field theory" that would provide the kind of clarity and order denied by Heisenberg's indeterminacy or uncertainty. He failed, and many critics have seen in his effort a dogmatism unworthy of Einstein's genius. The critics are wrong.

For what Einstein was up to was an act of faith that human knowing was more than a matter of probabilities. Asked why he believed in the brotherhood of man and the uniqueness of the individual, he once replied, "I believe [in these]. But if you ask me to prove what I believe, I can't. You know them to be true but you could spend a whole lifetime without being able to prove them.... There comes a point where the mind takes a leap to a higher plane of knowledge but can never prove how it got there. All great discoveries have involved such a leap"—including, of course, the discovery of God in human flesh, "wrapped in swaddling cloths and lying in a manger" (Lk 2:12).

Then there is curiosity, which may have killed the cat but is also an essential companion to the cardinal virtue of courage. Einstein again: "The important thing is not to stop questioning. Curiosity has its own reason for existing. One cannot help but be in awe when he contemplates the mysteries of eternity, of life, of the marvelous structure of reality. It is enough if one tries merely to comprehend a little of this mystery every day. Never lose a holy curiosity."

The world of the unrestrained pleasure principle is a world without windows or doors in which people are chained by appetites. Einstein, and the Vladimir Mother of God, remind us that we are not meant for narrowness—that in being bound and stretched by obligations freely undertaken, we pattern ourselves in the model of a crucified Redeemer who does not dissolve the problem of pain and evil, but nails himself, with us, to it.

California Dreamin', Missin' the Real Thing
Cass Elliott (1941–1974) and Denny Doherty (1940–2007)

Ah, the summer of 1967.

A gangly young Australian priest named George Pell came to my Baltimore parish on a circuitous route from ordination in Rome to graduate studies at Oxford and became a family friend; none of us imagined him the cardinal-archbishop of Sydney four decades hence, and the man later charged with cleaning up the Augean stables of Vatican finance.

Two June weeks in Chicago introduced me to Hyde Park, the Michigan dunes and the dubious pleasures of shoveling dead alewives off the beach, outdoor Shakespeare at the University of Chicago, Jerry and Dolores Freese, and a first romance.

Frank Robinson got hit in the head trying to break up a double play and couldn't see straight for months, and the World Champion Baltimore Orioles (not so puzzling a phrase then) tanked, a year after sweeping the Dodgers, Sandy Koufax, and Don Drysdale in the World Series.

Our fearsome English teacher assigned Paul Horgan's classic *Things As They Are* as one of the novels my incoming junior class was to read over the summer; thirty-eight years later, I'd write the introduction to a reprint edition of that underappreciated book. Gory Ohio State Highway Patrol movies were an integral part of drivers-ed, Jane Fonda led Robert Redford barefoot through the park, and Jim Brown didn't quite make it in *The Dirty Dozen*.

And there was the music. A lot of my Sixties memories have to do with the music, and the summer of '67 was no exception. The Association's "Windy" features prominently in my Lake Michigan beach memories. The 5th Dimension was heading up, up, and away in a beautiful balloon, while over in Motown, Aretha Franklin was demanding R-E-S-P-E-C-T. Lulu serenaded "Sir" (Sidney Poitier) with love; the Beatles traipsed down Penny Lane while Lucy was in the sky with diamonds; Billy Joe McAlister jumped off the Tallahatchie Bridge.

They didn't have a no. 1 hit that summer, but The Mamas and the Papas were very much in business, with the autobiographical "Creeque Alley" climbing to no. 5 on the U.S. charts and both "Twelve Thirty" and "My Girl" (a reprise of the Temptations' 1965 hit) brightening the summer of 1967's rock'n'roll scene. And brightening it was, because for tight harmony among beautifully matched voices, there was never anything quite like The Mamas and the Papas: John and Michelle Phillips, Denny Doherty, and Cass Elliot. Their songs still give me pleasure, which is more than I can say for other artifacts and memories of the Sixties.

It was all a huge mess, of course, and in ways a naive sixteen-year-old couldn't have imagined at the time (even though I thought I'd figured out some of the "Creeque Alley" references). One pop historian, quoted by Mark Steyn, summed up The Mamas and Papas' mess like this: "Before they hit the big time, the group dropped acid, smoked dope, and drank. After they hit the big time, the group dropped acid, smoked dope, and drank."

And as Steyn notes, respectfully if ironically, "To achieve that pure and translucent and cleanly harmonized a sound on that much hash, heroin, LSD, mescaline, and Black Beauties is quite an achievement."

The craziness eventually killed a way-too-young Cass Elliott, who died of a heart attack in 1974. But Mama Cass' heart had been broken before, when she fell in love with Papa Denny and he didn't reciprocate. (In fact, Denny had a torrid affair with Michelle Phillips that just about wrecked the group, even if it did produce a memorable song, "I Saw Her Again", in which Denny made the greatest false entrance in rock'n'roll history.) Cass Elliott was, of course, the fat one, the antithesis of sleek, blonde Michelle Phillips. But by all accounts, and even in her drug-addled condition, Cass really loved Denny Doherty. And as Steyn wrote in a fine obituary of Denny, "In his final years, widowed, weathered, balding, and paunchy, [Denny] conceded that turning her down was the great mistake of his life."

Why ponder all this, save for nostalgia's sake? Because the self-absorption of Sixties pop culture was its most soul-withering feature—more, in fact, than the drugs, the booze, the promiscuity, and the faux radicalism—all of which, on reflection, were either byproducts or expressions of that fascination (really, obsession) with Me. In the case of Denny Doherty and Cass Elliot, self-absorption was one big reason why the self-giving that makes real love possible was, well, impossible.

California dreamin' never made it to reality. And that's a great sadness.

The Doolittle Raiders

William Farrow (1918–1942), Dean Hallmark (1914–1942), and Robert Meder (1917–1943)

Like most denizens of Washington, I pay too little attention to the sites that other Americans make considerable sacrifices to visit. In the spring of 2015, prompted by reading James Scott's *Target Tokyo*, a comprehensive history of the famous Doolittle Raid of April 18, 1942, I strolled through Arlington National Cemetery on a bright, early spring afternoon in quest of three graves.

They were in section 12, side by side, each marked with a head-stone identical in its simplicity to so many thousands of others: William G. Farrow, Dean E. Hallmark, Robert J. Meder. Hallmark was the pilot of the sixth B-25 to take off from the pitching deck of USS *Hornet*, more than seven decades before; Meder was his co-pilot on the plane they christened *Green Hornet*. Farrow was the pilot of *Bat Out of Hell*, the last of the sixteen planes to roar down the flight deck of what President Franklin Roosevelt later called "our secret base at Shangri-La". Captured in Japanese-occupied China, Hallmark and Farrow were shot by their captors on October 15, 1942, after months of torture and deprivation and a bogus "trial"; Meder died of starvation in a Japanese prison on December 11, 1943. All three were cremated, their names deliberately falsified on the urns that bore their ashes. The urns were properly identified after the Japanese surrender and returned to the United States, where they now rest, sheltered under a tree, down the hill from the equally simple grave of the airmen's legendary commander, Jimmy Doolittle.

Target Tokyo is gut-wrenching in its description of what these men, and four of their fellow airmen whose death sentences were commuted to life imprisonment, suffered in Japanese prisons. One day, however, the imprisoned Doolittle Raiders were given an old Bible, which they began to share, taking turns reading in their cells. As Carroll Glines writes in *The Doolittle Raid*, "Up to this time, each man resorted to various methods to pass away hundreds of lonely hours.... [But] it was the Bible, they admitted unanimously later, that had a profound impact on their respective outlooks.... None of the four men would have called himself religious and none had ever read the Bible through before.... [Yet] they attributed their survival to the message of hope they found in its tattered pages."

That hope, I suspect, would not have been nourished so well had the imprisoned, emaciated Raiders been given *The Origin of Species* or *The Critique of Pure Reason*; a death-defying hope might not even have been nurtured by *David Copperfield* or *Pride and Prejudice*. It was the Psalms, the Hebrew prophets, and the Gospels that inspired in these men, living under extremities of cruelty that beggar the imagination, a life-sustaining hope; a willingness to forgive their captors; gratitude to God for their survival—and for one, a new vocation. Jacob DeShazer, the bombardier on Farrow's plane, became a Methodist missionary, returned to Japan, and converted Mitsuo Fuchida, the Japanese pilot who led the attack on Pearl Harbor, to Christianity.

Where did America get men like the Doolittle Raiders? Jimmy Doolittle was already a world-famous pilot (with a doctorate from MIT) when he talked his way into leading the raid that will forever bear his name. The seventy-nine other Raiders were known to few others except their families, friends, and fellow soldiers. The Hollywood gloss of *Thirty Seconds Over Tokyo* notwithstanding, they weren't all handsome and they weren't angelic. But they believed that their country was worth defending, and that its defense was worth risking their lives on a volunteer mission that wasn't even disclosed to them until *Hornet* passed beneath the Golden Gate Bridge, steaming west into harm's way.

I think it's safe to say that none of the Doolittle Raiders thought America an ill-founded republic or the source of the world's ills, although many of their families had struggled through the Great Depression. They were brave men and patriots, the products of an imperfect but intact public culture that nurtured millions of heroes like them. Standing under that tree in Arlington, I could only wonder what Bill Farrow, Dean Hallmark, and Bob Meder might say about American culture today.

The China Missioner
Francis X. Ford, M.M. (1892–1952)

In a 2010 interview with *Catholic World Report*, Cardinal Joseph Zen, S.D.B., the emeritus bishop of Hong Kong, wondered aloud about the Catholic Church's reticence to acknowledge those who had been martyred by Chinese communists during the Maoists' rise to power, and thereafter. "Why should we not publicize ... those martyrs?" Cardinal Zen asked. The truth demands it. Self-respect requires it. Today's Chinese Catholics, especially those who are persecuted for their fidelity to the Bishop of Rome, would be strengthened by the example of brave witnesses who held firm until the end, Zen suggested.

I think Cardinal Zen was entirely right. One way to start filling in the blanks of China's modern Catholic history would be to remember, and beatify, a martyred American missionary in China: Bishop Francis X. Ford, M.M.

Francis Ford, the first student to come to the new seminary of the Catholic Foreign Mission Society of America when the order was founded in 1911, was one of the initial band of Maryknoll missioners to go to China. Ordained a bishop in 1935, he made a point of training a native clergy to whom he could eventually entrust his diocese. Before that could happen, Ford was arrested by the Chinese communist authorities and died in prison in 1952. Seven months after his death, *Time* described the drama of his last days, and elements of his heroic life, relying on the testimony of Ford's secretary, Sister Joan Marie Ryan, M.M., who had been placed under house arrest after Bishop Ford had been arrested on false charges of espionage:

[Bishop Ford] ... though never tried, was ... publicly paraded, beaten, and degraded in some of the cities in which he had done mission work since 1918. In one town the mob which had gathered to beat him with sticks and stones became so fierce that Bishop Ford's Communist guards fled in terror. Though knocked to the ground again and again, Bishop Ford did his best to walk calmly through the streets till the guards returned. In another town his neck was bound with a wet rope which almost choked him as it dried and shrank. Another rope was made to trail from under his gown like a tail. To humiliate them both, the [communists] once forced him to undress before Sister Joan Marie. She caught a glimpse of Bishop Ford for the last time in February of this year [i.e., 1952], the month the [communists] now say he died. His once dark hair was completely white, his body so emaciated that another prisoner was carrying him "like a sack of potatoes."

Bishop Ford had neither courted martyrdom nor shirked it. On first arriving in China, he uttered this prayer: "Lord, make us the doorstep by which the multitudes may come to worship Thee, and if ... we are ground underfoot and spat upon and worn out, at least we ... shall become the King's Highway in pathless China." In 20 years, Francis Ford increased his flock from 9,000 to 20,000, built schools, hostels and churches. When World War II came, he stuck by his post, aiding Chinese guerillas, helping downed American airmen escape, relieving war refugees in distress.

In the early years of the new century, I inquired of the relevant authorities why there was no beatification cause for this brave man, who should certainly be Blessed Francis Ford. It turned out that the cause had indeed been introduced, but that Roman concerns about offending the Chinese government—which, it will be remembered, pitched a hissy fit when Pope John Paul II canonized over 120 Chinese martyrs (all of whom had died before China's communist period) during the Great Jubilee of 2000—had led to the process being put on hold. That later changed, but the cause continued to proceed at a glacial pace.

Such reticence (perhaps better, in this context, kowtowing) strikes me as a demeaning, self-inflicted wound to the Church's mission. The evangelical future of the Catholic Church in China depends in no small part on the heroic resistance of today's Chinese Catholics to governmental attempts to turn their local Church into a subsidiary of the Chinese Communist Party and the Chinese state. Those Catholics need the encouragement of a witness like that given by Francis Xavier Ford. His cause may proceed slowly, but his blood may yet prove to have paved the King's Highway into the Middle Kingdom.

The Black Prince
Bernardin Gantin (1922–2008)

Cardinal Bernardin Gantin of Benin was one of world Catholicism's noblemen.

Born in what was then the French colony of Dahomey in 1922, a mere forty years after the first Catholic missionaries had arrived in that West African land, Bernardin Gantin was ordained a priest in 1951, consecrated auxiliary bishop of Cotonou in 1956, and named archbishop of that city in 1960.

After participating in all four sessions of the Second Vatican Council, Archbishop Gantin was brought to Rome by Pope Paul VI to work at the Congregation for the Evangelization of Peoples (known to all Roman hands by its former name, *Propaganda Fide*, or "Prop" for short). He then became president of the Pontifical Council for Justice and Peace and was created cardinal in June 1977.

In the run-up to the conclaves of 1978, some imagined Gantin as the first pope from sub-Saharan Africa; he never thought of himself in those terms, and likely played a role in Karol Wojtyła's election as John Paul II. Some of the Great Electors of 1978, including Cardinal Franz König of Vienna, thought of the Polish intellectual Wojtyła as a bridge to the communist world, a kind of political pope. Cardinal Gantin and his fellow Africans thought in rather different terms: from their experience of him at Vatican II and at subsequent Synods, they admired the lucidity of Wojtyła's faith, the clarity of his defense of Catholic doctrine, and his humility.

The African cardinals—all new Christians—got the saint they wanted. The rest of us got a very different kind of "political pope" who dramatically reshaped the history of the late twentieth century by being a pastor and a moral witness.

John Paul, for his part, reposed enormous trust in Bernardin Gantin, appointing him prefect of the crucial Congregation for Bishops; and in 1993, he became dean of the College of Cardinals. It was in the latter roles that I first knew Gantin and was deeply impressed by his faith, his good humor, and his transparent integrity. Here, one thought, was a prince, long before he acquired the title; and he was a prince because he was a Christian, a man unafraid of the future because the future was assured by Christ.

One also sensed a deep spiritual bond between the Polish pope, saturated in a millennium of Christian history, and this child of the first modern African evangelization. The son of a retired soldier and the son of a railway worker, both from what some (including many curialists) regarded as the borderlands of the faith, came to the apostolic and administrative center of the Church and found in each other a devotion to Christ that transcended race, culture, and language. Both were also men of courage, whose fearlessness was another byproduct of faith. Thus Gantin, when swearing in new staff members at the Congregation for Bishops and receiving their promise of strict confidentiality about their work, gave each of them a picture of John Paul II collapsing in the popemobile after being shot on May 13, 1981. This, he seemed to be saying to those who worked for him, is what we are about: self-sacrifice.

In an oblique way that spoke volumes about the man's character, Cardinal Gantin was also one of those most responsible for the election of Joseph Ratzinger as Benedict XVI in 2005. On turning eighty in 2002, Gantin lost his vote in any future conclave. Neither canon law nor the apostolic constitution governing papal elections requires that a cardinal who reaches the age of eighty must thereby relinquish his post as dean of the College of Cardinals, however.

Bernardin Gantin was a man of great humility as well as integrity, and he seemed to think his brother cardinals, and the whole Church, would benefit from his stepping aside to allow the vice-dean, Cardinal Ratzinger, to succeed him. So Cardinal Gantin resigned as dean, returned home to Benin, and took up pastoral work.

Cardinal Gantin's self-effacing humility and profound churchmanship paved the way for Cardinal Ratzinger, as dean, to preside over the general congregations of cardinals that followed the death of John Paul II and to be the principal concelebrant and homilist at John Paul's funeral Mass. No one should doubt that Ratzinger's performance in those roles had a lot to do with the swift resolution of the conclave of 2005 in his favor. Thus did Gantin, a man who did not lack a sense of self but whose sense of self was not ego-driven, do a last great service for the universal Church.

It was an example that future deans might well emulate.

A Cardinal Conquering Pain

Francis Eugene George, O.M.I. (1937–2015)

Francis George was many things: a dedicated missionary priest; a serious intellectual; a shrewd analyst of public life; the first Chicago native to be named archbishop of the Windy City; a great national leader of the Church in the United States. But when word of his death came, a few days before I had hoped to have a last chance to speak with him in person, my first thought was that, in the Lord's mercy, he was no longer in pain.

His sister once told then-Father Robert Barron, a Chicago priest, that, if he wanted to understand her brother, he should remember that "he's always in pain." A polio survivor from the days of the iron lung, Francis George spent his entire adult life with his legs encased in dozens of pounds of steel. Then he was struck by bladder cancer and lived for years with what he called, ruefully, a "neobladder". He beat that challenge, but then another form of cancer struck and his last years were filled with new pain, more pain, different pain. Yet not once, since I first met him in the mid-1980s when he was Father Francis George, did I ever hear him complain about the pain—or about the sometimes strange ways that God has with those he has blessed in so many other facets of their lives.

Francis George could live in chronic pain because he conformed his life to Christ and the Cross. Death was his liberation from pain, not because pain gave way to oblivion, but because the Lord he served so long and well welcomed a good and faithful servant home, to a realm beyond pain.

Perhaps the most appropriate Gospel passage to ponder when thinking about lives like that of Cardinal George is the story of the Transfiguration. For in preserving the memory of the transfigured Christ, whose "face shone like the sun" and whose "garments became white as light" (Mt 17:2), the first generation of Christians bore witness to their hope for the human future. The transfigured Christ not only prefigured the Risen Christ, in whose Eastertide Francis George died; the transfigured Christ prefigures the life that awaits the friends of the Risen One in his Kingdom, at the Wedding Feast of the Lamb. There, there is no polio, and no post-polio syndrome. There, there is no cancer, no gut-wrenching chemotherapy, no catheters, no diminishment of vigor. There, there is only fullness of life, with palsied limbs made whole in a wholly new way.

That is the future in which Cardinal Francis George believed. That that is the future in which he shares is the consolation of those who loved and admired him.

Since its inception in 1789, the American hierarchy has not been noted for scholar-bishops—unlike, say, the Catholic Church in Germany. But in Francis Eugene George, the Catholic Church in the United States found itself with a leader of world-class intellect, with two earned doctorates yet with none of the intellectual deformities associated with the contemporary academy. He was, in the best sense of the term, a free thinker: one who thought independently of the reigning cultural shibboleths, yet within the tradition of the Church and its intellectual heritage. His was a thoroughly modern intellect; yet how appropriate that he died on the day when the Church reads the Johannine account of Jesus' feeding of the five thousand (6:1–15), with the Lord's admonition to "gather up the fragments left over, that nothing may be lost" (v. 12). For Cardinal George's fidelity to the tradition was in response to that admonition. He knew that the tradition had something to teach us today; he practiced what Chesterton called "the democracy of the dead".

That Johannine reference works in other ways, too. For when Francis George became archbishop of Chicago in 1997, there were a lot of fragments to be gathered up. Six months after his appointment, we were together in Rome and I asked him what he'd learned so far about what had long considered itself the flagship archdiocese of the United States. "I'm sixty years old," he said, "and in the fifteen years I've got left I've got to get people going back to Mass again and I've got to get priests hearing confessions again." He worked hard to do that and did so with effect. And if some of the notoriously difficult Chicago clergy never quite got it, a lot of the people of the Archdiocese of Chicago did—and in the brief months of his retirement, the cardinal remarked in our conversations on how touched he was by people coming up to him in parishes and thanking him for what he had done for the archdiocese.

What turned out to be our final meeting took place at Mundelein Seminary, which he had thoroughly reformed, in October 2014. (Something of the larger-than-life quality of old Chicago Catholicism can be gleaned from the story about the coat of arms of Cardinal George William Mundelein, founder of the seminary, which is carved into the altar of the seminary's main chapel. The motto on his arms read *Deus Adjutor Meus* [God Is My Help], which local clerical wags translated as "God Is My Auxiliary [Bishop]".) Father Robert Barron, then the rector, had built a new daily-Mass chapel for the growing seminary community. The chapel was to be dedicated to the newly canonized Pope Saint John Paul II, and Father Barron had invited me to give a public lecture on the late pope after Cardinal George consecrated the chapel—which he did, walking with difficulty on crutches, rubbing great swaths of holy chrism into the altar, and then celebrating the first Mass offered there. It was another example of Cardinal George's extraordinary physical courage—but he was determined to keep his commitment to consecrate the chapel, in no small part because of his love and esteem for John Paul II. At lunch afterward, he made unmistakably plain his concern about the direction that the pontificate of Pope Francis was taking and told me that he'd let the Pope know about it in a personal letter. Inquiring minds will wonder about the relationship of that letter to the appointment of Cardinal George's successor.

Like the Polish pope—another man determined to "gather up the fragments" and then re-knead them into a contemporary synthesis of Catholic faith and practice—Francis George was a keen observer (and critic) of the Western civilizational project. And his concerns about the trajectory on which that project seemed headed were neatly captured in a sound bite, excerpted from a lengthy discussion with his priests, in which the cardinal said that he expected to die in bed; he expected his successor to die in prison; and he expected the following archbishop of Chicago to be a martyr in the public square.

It was a deliberately provocative formulation, intended to get the priests of Chicago thinking seriously about the challenges posed by what Pope Benedict XVI had called the "dictatorship of relativism". To some it bespoke resignation, even surrender. That misimpression was due to the fact that the cardinal's hypothetical was always cut short in the reporting of it. For what he said, in full, was that he expected to die in bed; his successor would die in prison; that man's successor would be publicly executed; and *his* successor would "pick up the shards of a ruined society and slowly help rebuild civilization, as the Church has done so often in human history".

Like John Paul II, Francis George knew that the Catholic Lite project—the unhappy dumbing down of the vibrant, progressive, Chicago Catholicism of the 1930s and 1940s—was unfit to fight the zeitgeist in the name of freedom rightly understood, or to "gather up the fragments" and help rebuild the American experiment after the zeitgeist had done its worst. But it would be a great disservice to his memory to suggest that Francis George was at war with "liberal" Catholicism. In the first place, he refused to think of the Church as something that could be defined in terms of "liberal" or "conservative". As he said at his first Chicago press conference in 1997, the Church is about true and false, not Left and Right. Moreover, he knew that Catholic Lite was dying of its own implausibility, so why waste energy battling it? Rather, "gather up the fragments"— including the fragments of good in the once-vital reform Catholicism of Chicago—and get on with the task of reevangelizing both the Church and the Great American City.

That could be done, the cardinal was convinced, only by what you might call All-In Catholicism: a Church that offered both mercy and truth; a Church that was both pro-life and committed to the effective empowerment of the poor; a Church that could make Catholicism compelling in a culture that was too often simply indifferent to what religious communities had to say. That apathy would not be met by surrendering to the fashions of the age core Catholic understandings of what makes for human happiness. But neither would it be met by argument alone. Arguments were important, this man of intellect and culture knew; so was witness, and that was why he put such energy into defending the Church's institutions for empowering the poor— its schools, health-care facilities, and social-service centers—against the encroachments of a government trying to use the Church for its own purposes.

When the U.S. bishops elected Cardinal George their president in 2007, they underscored a profound change in the dynamics of

Catholic life in America. The liveliest centers of Catholicism in America—the parishes, the dioceses, the seminaries, the lay renewal movements, the growing orders of consecrated religious life—are those that have embraced what John Paul II called the "New Evangelization". The course into the future has been set. Francis George helped set that course. When it comes time to write his story in full, he will be remembered as the most consequential archbishop of Chicago in the modern history of the Church—and a leader in American Catholicism whose intellectual and physical courage was instrumental in making the Church in the United States, for all its challenges and problems, the most vital in the developed world.

He is now without pain, whole and healed. Francis George has met Christ the Lord and is living in the presence of the Thrice-Holy God—to whom I give thanks for his life, his witness, and our friendship.

The "Loud-Mouthed Irish Priest"
Andrew M. Greeley (1928–2013)

Let me begin by paying Father Andrew Greeley a compliment he'd never have paid me, or indeed anyone of my "location" in the Church: Catholicism in the United States was a lot duller after Greeley was felled by an accident in 2008, and the Church has felt emptier since his death in 2013.

In the first decades of his remarkably busy career, Greeley did serious academic work in sociology, taking down a number of shibboleths about Catholic culture and Catholic schools and demonstrating empirically the educational, professional, and financial upward mobility of white Catholic ethnics in the United States. At the same time, Greeley ground out several useful books of popular apologetics that "translated" post–Vatican II theology into a language accessible to nonspecialists. He also pioneered the "conclave book" with *The Making of the Popes 1978*, establishing a model I hope I improved in 2005 with *God's Choice*. His seemingly innumerable novels sold like hotcakes; prior to his getting involved in fiction, it was often said that Andy had never had an unpublished thought, and after a few lowbrow-popular bodice-rippers, some were uncharitable enough to add "and never an unpublished fantasy".

For decades, Greeley was the beau ideal of many in the Catholic columnizing business, and when he finally downed tools on that front, my own column the following week was a lament for a feisty writer's departure from the lists. He sent a letter of thanks, the bulk of which consisted of complaints that no one else had bothered to thank him for grinding out so many columns over the years. Later, it struck me that this was one key to Greeley's complex personality: for all of his self-conscious brashness, he very much wanted to be accepted, especially by bishops, a class he excoriated regularly.

We only met twice, during the 2005 papal interregnum. I warmly welcomed him to our makeshift NBC "newsroom" when he came up to the Janiculum Hill to do the *Today* program; we talked about my daughter Monica's affection for Chicago, which Greeley described winsomely as "an easy city to love". A few nights later, I found Andy and his secretary in the glory that was "Armando's", a trattoria near the Vatican that was the nocturnal GHQ for Father Richard John Neuhaus, Father Raymond de Souza, Raymond Arroyo, and others of our gang. Andy and I exchanged a few pleasantries about how things had changed in the Church since 1978 and the year of three popes; I'd rather hold on to that recollection of him than the memory of my surprise a year later when, in his own book on the 2005 papal transition, he went out of his way to put down my friends and me as "the Scary Guys" (i.e., supporters of John Paul II who didn't fit the liberal stereotype of grumpy, troglodytic conservatives).

That snarkiness was of a piece with Greeley's failure to "get" John Paul II, which likely had a lot to do with Andy's consistent, indeed obsessive, deprecation of *Humanae Vitae*, Paul VI's encyclical on regulating fertility. For Greeley, *Humanae Vitae* was the great disaster of postconciliar Catholicism; that conviction was like a set of blinders, obscuring his view of other realities in the Church. Thus, insofar as I'm aware, Greeley never took the measure of John Paul II's Theology of the Body, although the Polish pope's creative wrestling with the theological and moral meaning of our being made male and female would seem to be of a piece with Greeley's insistence on the sacramental goodness of sex within the bond of marriage. But John Paul didn't throw *Humanae Vitae* over the side of the Barque of Peter; so in the Greeley taxonomy of matters Catholic, John Paul II had to be a bad guy, if of the "great missed opportunity" sort of bad guy.

Walking through the hallways of Chicago's Mundelein Seminary after giving a lecture there, I came across the picture of the ordination class of 1954, and there was Andy: airbrushed, according to the photographic custom of the day, and looking for all the world like Bing Crosby in *Going My Way* and *The Bells of St. Mary's*. Which seems about right: for Andrew Moran Greeley embodied in a singular way the last rowdy moment of urban, ethnic, Counter-Reformation Catholicism in America. He once described himself as just a "loud-mouthed Irish priest", a sobriquet that certainly captured at least one facet of his oversized personality. He didn't get the Evangelical Catholicism of John Paul II, nor did he understand that the Church of the New Evangelization was what Vatican II was really all about. So in an ironic way, this quintessential old-school Catholic liberal was a man of the past.

But his work sure gave Team Liberal in the Catholic Counter-Reformation League a boisterous ninth inning.

James Madison Meets Frank Zappa
Václav Havel (1936–2011)

Václav Havel, who died on December 18, 2011, was one of the great contemporary exponents of freedom lived nobly. His moral mettle proved true in both the world of ideas and the world of affairs; indeed, few men in post–World War II European public life moved more surely between those two worlds. In that respect, and for his personal courage, Havel reminded me of one of the American Founders—if, that is, one could imagine John Adams or James Madison hanging out with Frank Zappa.

After his death, Havel's brilliant literary deconstruction of the moral tawdriness of late bureaucratic communism, the underground essay called "The Power of the Powerless", was widely and appropriately quoted. Another Havel essay from his days in opposition also bears rereading: "The Anatomy of a Reticence", the Czech playwright's 1985 critique of the willful blindness of Western peace activists about the nature of Soviet totalitarianism. Both Havel masterpieces continue to speak to us today about the dangers of political conformity and the dangers of political utopianism.

Two decades into the twenty-first century, as the United States finds itself in a season of profound political discontent and snark has replaced smarts as the political coin of the realm, President Havel's January 1, 1990, speech also bears close study. The "Velvet Revolution" that deposed Czechoslovak communism had swept Havel into Hradčany Castle three days before. Here is some of what the man who had spent much of 1989 in a communist prison said to his countrymen in his first New Year's Day address as their president:

My dear fellow citizens:
For forty years you heard from my predecessors on this day different variations on the same theme: how our country was flourishing,

how many million tons of steel we produced, how happy we all were, how we trusted our government, and what bright perspectives were unfolding in front of us. I assume you did not propose me to this office so that I, too, would lie to you.

Our country is not flourishing. The enormous creative and spiritual potential of our nations is not being used sensibly. Entire branches of industry are producing goods that are of no interest to anyone, while we are lacking the things we need. A state which calls itself a workers' state humiliates and exploits workers. . . .

But [the economic mess] is still not the main problem. The worst thing is that we live in a contaminated moral environment. We fell morally ill because we became used to saying something different from what we thought. We learned not to believe in anything, to ignore one another, to care only about ourselves. Concepts such as love, friendship, compassion, humility, or forgiveness lost their depth and dimension, and for many of us they represented only psychological peculiarities, or they resembled gone-astray feelings from ancient times, a little ridiculous in the era of computers and spaceships. . . .

When I talk about the contaminated moral atmosphere . . . I am talking about all of us. We had all become used to the totalitarian system and accepted it as an unchangeable fact and thus helped perpetuate it. In other words, we are all—though naturally to different extents—responsible for the operation of the totalitarian machinery. None of us is just its victim. We are all also its co-creators.

Why do I say this? It would be very unreasonable to understand the sad legacy of the last forty years as something alien, which some distant relative bequeathed to us. On the contrary, we have to accept this legacy as a sin we committed against ourselves. If we accept it as such, we will understand that it is up to us all, and up to us alone, to do something about it. We cannot blame the previous rulers for everything, not only because it would be untrue, but also because it would blunt the duty that each of us faces today: namely, the obligation to act independently, freely, reasonably and quickly. . . . Freedom and democracy include participation and therefore responsibility from us all.

Vaclav Havel had a complicated relationship with the Catholic Church. But his remarks on the arrival of Pope John Paul II in Prague in 1990 made abundantly clear that his noble human spirit was, ultimately, grounded in his faith in a divine Spirit:

Your Holiness, my dear fellow citizens:

I am not sure that I know what a miracle is. In spite of this, I dare say that, at this moment, I am participating in a miracle: the man who six months ago was arrested as an enemy of the State stands here today as the president of that State, and bids welcome to the first Pontiff in the history of the Catholic Church to set foot in this land.

I am not sure that I know what a miracle is. In spite of this, I dare say that this afternoon I shall participate in a miracle: in the same place where, five months ago, on the day in which we rejoiced over the canonization of Agnes of Bohemia, when the future of our country was decided, today the head of the Catholic Church will celebrate Mass and will probably thank our saint for her intercession before him who holds in his hand the inscrutable course of all things.

I am not sure I know what a miracle is. In spite of this, I dare say that at this moment I am participating in a miracle: in a country devastated by the ideology of hatred, the messenger of love has arrived; in a country devastated by the government of the ignorant, the living symbol of culture has arrived; in a country which until a short time ago was devastated by the idea of confrontation and division in the world, the messenger of peace, dialogue, mutual tolerance, esteem and calm understanding, the messenger of fraternal unity in diversity, has arrived.

During these long decades, the Spirit was banished from our country. I have the honor of witnessing the moment in which its soil is kissed by the apostle of spirituality.

Welcome to Czechoslovakia, Your Holiness.

Havel's moral clarity, his bracing honesty about the effects of a common failure to live freedom nobly, and his conviction that faith in God enlarges the human spirit are all desperately needed in the mid-twenty-first-century West, not least in the United States. Brave men and women found it possible to live in the truth in the late twentieth century. The course of the twenty-first will depend on whether we learn from their example—or ignore it.

The Clear-Eyed Phenomenologist
Dietrich von Hildebrand (1889–1977)

Dietrich von Hildebrand, who saw a lot in almost nine decades of academic and public life before his death in 1977, was a German Catholic philosopher, part of a circle of thinkers that first formed around Edmund Husserl, founder of the philosophical method known as "phenomenology". Others in that circle included Max Scheler, on whom Karol Wojtyła (Saint John Paul II) wrote his second doctoral thesis, and Edith Stein, now Saint Teresa Benedicta of the Cross. The phenomenologists thought that philosophy had gotten detached from reality, drifting into the quicksand of thinking-about-thinking-about-thinking. Their motto was "to the things themselves", and their project was to reconnect thought to reality by a precise observation and analysis of Things As They Are.

Phenomenology, alas, also rates a shrine in the philosophy wing of the Opacity Hall of Fame. The phenomenological method lends itself to a certain circularity of expression, and a lot of patience is required to work through a typically dense phenomenological text—especially when the author is German. In my brief experience of him as a philosopher, Dietrich von Hildebrand was no exception to this rule.

Imagine my happy surprise, then, in discovering a collection of Hildebrand's diaries and pre–World War II lectures, edited and translated by John Henry Crosby and John F. Crosby and published under the title *My Battle Against Hitler: Faith, Truth, and Defiance in the Shadow of the Third Reich*. Here was a Hildebrand I'd never met before: a crisp, feisty writer who wore his emotions on his literary sleeve as he fought against the emerging Hitler regime and battled the Catholic intellectuals who were seduced by it, some for brief periods, others for longer.

That seduction was, in a word, appalling. In May 1933, for example, the Catholic Academic Association met at the Benedictine Abbey of Maria Laach (one of the centers of the pre–Vatican II Liturgical

Movement). To what Hildebrand described as his "great distress", Hitler's vice chancellor, Franz von Papen, a Catholic, was invited to lecture; even worse, "a priest from Maria Laach praised the Third Reich as the realization of the Body of Christ in the secular world". Hildebrand resigned from the association to protest this "ignominious affair".

Dietrich von Hildebrand believed that Nazism breathed the ancient spirit of the Antichrist, with whom the Church could have no truck. Thus he wrote to friends in Munich at Pentecost 1933, explaining that "it is completely immaterial if the Antichrist refrains from attacking the Church for political reasons, or if he concludes a Concordat with the Vatican. What is decisive is the spirit that animates him, the heresy he represents, the crimes committed at his behest. God is offended regardless of whether the victim of murder is a Jew, a Socialist, or a bishop. Blood that has been innocently spilled cries out to heaven."

Why did intelligent Catholics in Germany and elsewhere fall prey to the siren songs of German National Socialism? A close reading of Hildebrand's diaries suggests that it was in part because they despised liberal democracy, which they regarded as "bourgeois" and decadent. And there certainly were elements of decadence and aggressive secularism in Germany's interwar Weimar Republic, as the hit Broadway show and movie *Cabaret* remind us.

But a Catholic answer to the quandaries of political modernity was not going to be found in Hitler's Third Reich (which some foolishly imagined the forerunner of a new Holy Roman Empire) or in Mussolini's Fascism (which some Catholics thought an expression of the "corporatism" espoused by Pope Pius XI's 1931 social encyclical, *Quadragesimo Anno*). The answer was a democracy (even under a constitutional monarch) tethered to moral truth through a religiously informed public philosophy drawn from Europe's heritage of reason and revelation—from the legacies left to Europe by Athens and Jerusalem.

As I read the Hildebrand diaries, it became depressingly obvious that that option—which would become the social teaching of the Church under John Paul II and Benedict XVI—was not on the table when European Catholic scholars discussed the crisis of their continent during the Great Depression. The same blind spot was also evident in some *soi-disant* radical Catholics of the interwar era like the French publicist Emmanuel Mounier. This was more than a failure of intellectual and political imagination, however. By failing to provide the intellectual ballast for a broad-based, effective, coherent, and thoroughly Catholic opposition to the Nazi claim to have solved the problems of social solidarity and political cohesion in modernity, blind Catholic intellectuals besotted by abstractions played a tragic role in helping make possible the catastrophes of the Second World War and the Holocaust. And in doing so, they helped pave the way toward Europe's current moral-cultural sclerosis.

There are lessons here for all, but especially for those twenty-first-century "Radical Catholics", "Traditional Catholics", and "integralists" tempted to turn legitimate critiques of democratic practice into contempt for the democratic experiment *in se*. Dietrich von Hildebrand, whose determination to speak the truth about the things he saw clearly drove him into exile, is thus an important teacher for a century he never lived to see, but some of whose challenges he would have quickly recognized.

The Exile Become National Hero
Lubomyr Husar, M.S.U. (1933–2017)

How does it happen that a child growing up in eastern Galicia among Ukrainians, Poles, Moldovans, Germans, Austrians, Jews, Roma, and Armenians dodges Nazi death squads and the Red Army, learns firsthand what it means to be a "displaced person" in occupied Austria, immigrates to the United States, completes university and seminary studies before being ordained a priest, writes a groundbreaking doctoral dissertation on ecumenism, joins a monastic order, is illicitly ordained a bishop, has his episcopal ordination recognized by Saint John Paul II, is created a cardinal by the same pope—and at an age when many men begin to contemplate retirement, returns to his newly self-liberated homeland for the first time in a half-century, and, over the next two decades, becomes the most widely respected and deeply beloved figure in the country?

To comprehend the extraordinary life of Cardinal Lubomyr Husar, M.S.U., who rose to become major archbishop of Kyiv-Halych, is to trace the arc of the slow-motion martyrdom of the Ukrainian Greek Catholic Church in the mid-twentieth century and that Eastern Catholic Church's resurrection in the twenty-first.

As the Catholic Church in Poland was the safe deposit box of national memory and identity during the 123 years when "Poland" disappeared from the map of Europe (having been vivisected by Russia, Austria, and Prussia in the Third Polish Partition of 1795), so the Ukrainian Greek Catholic Church (UGCC) was one of the principal repositories of Ukrainian national identity and aspiration in the hard decades when Stalin first tried to starve Ukraine into submission and later used every tool at the disposal of a totalitarian state to destroy Ukraine's language, culture, and self-awareness—a project continued for almost four decades by Stalin's successors. But an argument can be made that the achievement of the UGCC in Ukraine was even more remarkable than that of the Latin-Rite Catholic Church in Poland.

For Polish Catholicism was very much a visible presence in Poland's national life, both during the partitions that eradicated the country and, later, under both Nazi and communist tyranny. The UGCC, however, did its most impressive work of preserving and developing national identity, culture, and morale during the four and a half decades when it was the world's largest illegal religious body—when it was an underground Church with no public presence whatsoever, thanks to a canonically illicit and coerced "reunion" with Russian Orthodoxy engineered in 1946 by the Soviet secret police and the leadership of the Russian Orthodox Church. And while the UGCC hung on by its collective fingernails between 1946 and 1991, conducting clandestine worship and education in the Ukrainian forests, Ukrainian Greek Catholic leaders like Lubomyr Husar, living in the West—in Husar's case, in New York, Washington, and other American locales, before redeploying to Rome—laid the foundations for a revival of Greek Catholic life at a time that, for most of Husar's adult life, seemed unimaginable: the time of an independent Ukraine unshackled from the Soviet Union and free to create its own destiny.

That hoped-for miracle of liberation took place in 1991 when the Soviet Union dissolved, and since then, Greek Catholic life in Ukraine has flourished. Lubomyr Husar, a man of deep faith, would be the first to insist that that miraculous resurrection was a work of divine providence and grace. But Cardinal Husar (who was buried in the Patriarchal Cathedral of the Resurrection of Christ in Kyiv after hundreds of thousands of his countrymen paid him their last respects in the days after his death) should be given full marks for his vision and wisdom: for he was a remarkable character who bridged numerous worlds—Byzantine and Latin, Catholic and Orthodox, religious and secular, premodern and postmodern—in a singular way.

It was Husar who staunchly supported the development of the Ukrainian Catholic University, the only Catholic institution of higher learning in the former Soviet space, which in a mere two decades has become one of the premier universities in Ukraine and a model for higher education unburdened by the intellectual and moral corruptions of *Homo Sovieticus*. It was Husar, as head of the UGCC, who oversaw an extraordinary expansion of the Greek Catholic priesthood and saw to the reform of seminaries so that the clergy of an independent Ukraine would be better equipped to minister in a post-underground religious environment. It was Husar who welcomed John Paul II to Ukraine in 2001—a weeklong pilgrimage that, against all the odds and most expectations, became a moment of ecumenical encounter between Greek Catholics and Ukrainian Orthodox.

And it was Husar who, in retirement, became a moral reference point for a society still deeply wounded by its Soviet past. In a country struggling to shed the bad habits of duplicity engrained during its communist period, and in a political community whose debates were (and are) often more characterized by heat than light, Lubomyr Husar became a kind of national patriarch: the voice of reason, moderation, and wise counsel amidst the cacophony of postcommunist politics. And during the Maidan protests in 2013–2014 (the Revolution of Dignity), a now-blind Cardinal Husar could be found on Kyiv's Independence Square, in solidarity with his people's hopes for a future beyond corruption, a future in which Ukraine would take its rightful place as an integral part of the West, bringing with it the riches of Byzantine spirituality and culture.

That the UGCC was led after Husar by a dynamic young successor, Major Archbishop Sviatoslav Shevchuk, is another testimony to Husar's leadership, for he raised up a generation of polyglot, intellectually well-prepared, and politically shrewd leaders such as Shevchuk and the founding president of the Ukrainian Catholic University, Borys Gudziak, who in 2019 became the Ukrainian Greek Catholic metropolitan archbishop of Philadelphia. Like Cardinal Husar, whom they revered, Shevchuk and Gudziak are men of God who have played and will continue to play an indispensable public role in a twenty-first-century Ukraine struggling to realize the bright promise of the Maidan revolution while suffering under a Russian invasion that cost over ten thousand lives and created more than a million and a half internally displaced persons. It was likely a sadness to Husar that the Vatican never brought itself to use the words "invasion" and "illegal annexation" to describe the Russian occupation of Crimea, or the word "war" to describe what Russia was doing in eastern Ukraine from 2014 on. But Ukrainian Catholic leaders have long been accustomed to finding their loyalty to Rome poorly repaid by a Holy See in thrall to the fantasy of a grand *rapprochement* with Russian Orthodoxy.

A rethinking of the Vatican's misadventures in *Ostpolitik* would be a fitting tribute to Cardinal Husar. But whatever happens along the Tiber, the remarkable life of Lubomyr Husar helped make it possible for the Ukrainian Greek Catholic Church to thrive in an independent Ukraine. "Freedom," Husar insisted, "is the opportunity to do good." That, he did. May his memory be eternal.

The Majesty of the Rule of Law

Henry J. Hyde (1924–2007)

In September 1984, I began a sabbatical year at Washington's Wood-row Wilson International Center for Scholars. One day that month, while I was having lunch with a Seattle-area congressman, Joel Pritchard, then in the midst of a round of chemotherapy, a portly gentleman came up to our table in the dining room of the House of Representatives to ask Joel how he was feeling. Congressman Pritchard introduced me to Congressman Henry Hyde, who politely asked what I was doing in town. I explained that I was exploring Catholic thought on war and peace at the Wilson Center. Hyde smiled and went off to his own lunch.

Fifteen minutes later, he came back and asked me, "Have you ever written anything on Church and state?" I replied that I had and would be happy to send him some things, which I did. As it turned out, Hyde had been asked to give a lecture at the Notre Dame Law School in response to the "I'm personally opposed, but ..." abortion politics of Mario Cuomo and Geraldine Ferraro. (Note to younger readers: Cuomo was a three-term governor of New York; Ferraro was the vice-presidential candidate on a ticket that carried one state and the District of Columbia.) So I pitched in with the drafting of the speech, which was intended both as a rebuttal to Cuomoism and as a positive statement of how Catholic understandings of the dignity of the human person should engage the public square—a phrase then just coming into the national vocabulary.

From such an accidental beginning came one of the great friend-ships of my life and a twenty-year collaboration that would teach me a lot about how American politics really works (and doesn't).

Henry Hyde was, without exaggeration, a singularity. As Clement Attlee once said of Winston Churchill, Henry's personality resembled a layer cake. There was the Hyde who reveled in the contact sport that is Illinois politics and who regaled friends with Mr. Dooley-like stories of campaign shenanigans and naughtiness on both sides of the partisan divide. And there was the Hyde who was a close student of history, one of the most avid readers in the House of Representatives.

There was the Hyde who was the undisputed legislative leader of the American pro-life movement, the man who almost single-handedly kept the federal treasury from funding Big Abortion. And there was the Hyde who defied some conservative orthodoxies by arguing that it was nonsensical to claim that the Second Amendment created a constitutional right for eighteen-year-olds to own AK-47s and other assault weapons.

There was the Hyde whom Cokie Roberts (no conservative) once described to me as "the smartest man in Congress". And there was the Hyde who was one of the best joke-tellers of all time.

There was Hyde, the ambitious politician. And there was the Hyde who passed up what would turn out, later, to be a chance to become Speaker of the House, because he had given his word to minority leader Bob Michel to vote for Michel's candidate for whip.

There was the Hyde who was a master of rhetorical cut and thrust, the greatest extemporaneous debater in the House in his day. And there was the Hyde whom Nancy Pelosi and other similarly situated solons liked, respected, and perhaps even came to love.

One indelible memory that captures Henry Hyde in full involved Thanksgiving 1986. Henry's prostate was giving him grief, so he spent the holiday in Georgetown University Hospital. When I went to visit him on Thanksgiving Day, I found him sitting up in bed, tubes running in and out of him, smoking a six-inch-long cigar, watching TV as his beloved Chicago Bears played the Detroit Lions—and reading a massive tome on William Wilberforce, the British parliamentary scourge of the slave trade. I asked Henry whether he'd had a lot of visitors. He replied that a guy who was interested in running for his seat had come in and expressed grave concern. Said Henry, in a growling whisper, "I told him, 'The last words you'll ever hear me say are gonna be, "Get your foot off the oxygen hose." ' "

He loved the U.S. House of Representatives, and, while he made important contributions to foreign policy as one who married a profound concern for international human rights to a principled anticommunism, I think Henry most enjoyed chairing the Judiciary Committee after the Republicans took control of the House in January 1995. His remarks during the committee's first meeting under his chairmanship are worth remembering:

> In our American system, justice is not an abstraction. Like all the virtues, justice is a moral habit; we become a just society by acting justly. The duty to "promote justice," which we lay upon ourselves when we pledge to defend the Constitution, is a duty we exercise through the instrument of the law. [For] the "rule of law" distinguishes civilized societies from barbarism.
>
> That simple phrase—"the rule of law"—should lift our hearts. To be sure, it has little of the evocative power of Lincoln's call to rebuild a national community with "malice toward none" and "charity for all"; to celebrate the "rule of law" may stir our souls less than MacArthur's moving call to "Duty, Honor, Country." But if that phrase lacks the eloquence of Lincoln and MacArthur, it nonetheless calls us to a noble way of life.
>
> Legislators—makers of laws in a democratic republic—are involved in a vital task. Ours is not just a job; public service in the Congress is not just a career. What we do here we ought to do as a matter of vocation: as a matter of giving flesh and blood to our convictions about justice—our moral duty to give everyone his due. I have been in public life long enough to know that not every moment in politics is filled with nobility. But I have also been in public life long enough to know that those who surrender to cynicism and deny any nobility to the making of the laws end up doing grave damage to the rule of law—and to justice. If we don't believe that what we are doing here can rise above the brokering of raw interests—if we do not believe that politics and the making of the law can contribute to the ennobling of American democracy—then we have no moral claim to a seat in the Congress of the United States.

It was a touching confession of political faith, and Henry's conclusion was met with applause and cheers. Even such sworn partisan foes as the ranking minority member, John Conyers, and the ultraprochoice Patricia Schroeder were moved and leaned over to shake the new chairman's hand. (Chuck Schumer, if memory serves, continued to eat a jelly doughnut while chatting on the dais with his friend Howard Berman of California.)

In less than four years' time, of course, chairing the Judiciary Committee got Henry embroiled in the impeachment inquiry against

President Clinton. Hyde was a model of fairness throughout, as even a Clinton defender like Barney Frank acknowledged. His own falls from grace, decades in the past, were dredged up by reporters, aided and abetted (I am convinced) by unscrupulous Clintonistas, all of whom somehow imagined that the impeachment inquiry was about extracurricular sex. Henry was hurt, badly, and even talked of resigning. I remember telling him that no two people I had ever met had been more married than he and Jeanne (who had died in 1992), and that he owed it both to her forgiveness and his duty to press ahead. Which he did, in the conviction that President Clinton had put the Congress and the country in an impossible position. How could the nation have as its highest law-enforcement official a man guilty of a crime—perjury—for which more than a hundred other men and women were serving time in federal prisons?

When the House managers solemnly carried the Articles of Impeachment across the Capitol to the Senate, Henry Hyde saw in Trent Lott's eyes (as he told me later that night) that "we're not going to make it; Trent won't fight." Rather than let the trial of the president descend into farce, Henry tried heroically, through the force of argument and rhetoric, to keep the country focused on the nobility of the rule of law, as he did in opening the Senate trial for the House managers:

> Every senator in this chamber has taken an oath to do impartial justice under the Constitution. The president of the United States took an oath to tell the truth, the whole truth, and nothing but the truth in his testimony before the grand jury, just as he had, on two occasions, sworn a solemn oath to "faithfully execute the laws of the United States."
>
> The case before you, Senators, is about the taking of oaths: the president's oaths, and your own oaths. That is why your judgment must rise above politics, above partisanship, above polling data. This case is a test of whether what the Founding Fathers described as "sacred honor" still has meaning in these United States: two hundred twenty-two years after those words—sacred honor—were inscribed in our national charter of freedom....
>
> In recent months, it has often been asked—it has too often been asked—so what? What is the harm done by this lying, by this perjury? The answer would have been clear to those who once pledged their sacred honor to the cause of liberty. The answer would have been clear to those who crafted the world's most enduring constitution.

And the answer should be clear to us, the heirs of Washington, Jefferson, and Adams, Madison, Hamilton, and Jay.

No greater harm can be done than breaking the covenant of trust
between the president and the people; among the three branches of
our government; and between the country and the world. For to
break that covenant of trust is to dissolve the mortar that binds the
foundation stones of our freedom into a secure and solid edifice. And
to break the covenant of trust by violating one's oath is to do grave
damage to the rule of law among us.

The Senate acquitted the president by failing to reach the two-
thirds majority necessary for conviction, but students of American
history will read Henry Hyde's remarks during the impeachment
inquiry and trial for decades after President Clinton's memoir (with
its bitter criticisms of Hyde) is pulped.

Late in the Reagan years, hyperpartisan Democratic House Speaker
Jim Wright asked Henry to speak at a luncheon that Wright was
hosting for newly elected Members of Congress. Henry graciously
congratulated the neophyte legislators, cracked a few jokes, and then
got very serious. "You are basking in the glow of victory," he told
them, "and that is entirely understandable. But permit me to suggest,
on the basis of long experience, that if you don't know what you're
prepared to lose your seat for, you're going to do a lot of damage up
here. You have to know what you're willing to lose everything for
if you're going to be the kind of Member of Congress this country
needs." That was Henry Hyde. Even his most bitter political foes
knew that he spoke the truth, and that he meant it.

Once, addressing the National Right to Life Convention, Henry
reminded the ground troops of the pro-life movement that they were
not "playing to the gallery, but to the angels, and to Him who made
the angels". When he died on November 29, 2007, I imagined the
angels giving him a rousing Chicago-style welcome. So, I expect, did
today's holy innocents, the unborn, whose cause he championed for
decades with wisdom, wit, and effect. It seems too much to ask that
we'll ever see his like again. How blessed we were, as a nation under
God and under the rule of law, to have had his services for so long.

The Last Adult

Henry M. Jackson (1912–1983)

In his classic essay on Tolstoy, Sir Isaiah Berlin parsed the difference between two human archetypes, which he dubbed the "hedgehog" and the "fox". Most of us, Berlin argued, are foxes: we're interested in many things, driven by no one compelling passion, content to bounce from issue to issue and concern to concern, often too busy to worry about how it all fits together. The hedgehog, by contrast, is slower, more ungainly, much less romantic. But the hedgehog knows one great thing and sticks doggedly to that truth, in and out of season, to both praise and criticism. A world composed of hedgehogs would not be a very attractive, or even healthy, place. But a world without hedgehogs is perhaps in even greater peril.

Senator Henry M. Jackson, known to one and all as "Scoop", was a hedgehog in an era dominated by political foxes. The one great truth he knew—that totalitarianism was the most dangerous form of tyranny known to human history, and that that the Soviet Union uniquely incarnated the totalitarian anti-ethic—was popular in the 1950s when Jackson first came to national attention, unpopular in the late 1960s and 1970s when he ran for the presidency, and on the comeback in the 1980s when Jackson died prematurely, at the height of his powers and, perhaps, of his influence. And in a savage historical irony, Jackson died at precisely the moment when the truth of his convictions about the nature of Soviet power was demonstrated again, as the USSR sacrificed the lives of 269 innocent travelers on the altar of its paranoia, in the shootdown of Korean Airlines flight 007.

The consistency of Scoop's resolute anticommunism was certainly a factor in costing him the presidency. For in an age dominated by the politics of accommodation, Henry Jackson, whose intellect was far keener than his rhetorical powers, could come across as someone like the legendary minister who once harangued a congregation about the evils of sin and the pains of hell. After an hour or more of fire and brimstone, the preacher ended with the familiar Gospel text, "There will be weeping and gnashing of teeth" (Lk 13:28, KJV). At which point an old woman said in a loud stage whisper, "But I don't have any teeth ..." To which the minister instantly replied, "Teeth will be provided!" That was how an increasingly Left-leaning national media portrayed Scoop from the late 1960s on: Jackson as an anticommunist fundamentalist, the last Cold Warrior, the consummate hawk.

There could be no doubt about the depth of Jackson's anticommunism and his firm conviction that the survival of democracy required a stable, effective military shield against Soviet aggression. But to reduce Jackson's worldview to the bumper-sticker level of "consummate hawk" was to indulge in laziness, ignorance, or political malice. For throughout his entire public life, Henry M. Jackson remained a liberal internationalist. And as I came to know him and do some work with him in the last years of his life, it struck me that it was in the context of his liberal internationalism that his anticommunism ought to have been understood.

Like the forces in the American trade union movement with which he was long allied, Jackson knew that an exclusively military response to Soviet power, especially in Third World arenas where social change was imperative, was bound to fail. In the early 1980s, and against a great deal of opposition, Jackson brought that conviction to bear on the bloody mess that was Central America. Scoop clearly understood the Soviets' stake in a destabilized, even Marxist-dominated, Central America—a judgment vindicated in the decades after his death by newly available files from the Soviet secret intelligence service, the KGB, which documented not only Soviet involvement in Central American guerilla movements but Soviet penetration (and indeed sponsorship) of American activist organizations opposed to Reagan administration policy in the region. But Jackson also insisted that the "security shield" the United States should help build in Central America should be shielding genuine social, economic, and political reform, not reinforcing the power of the region's oligarchs.

Those who dismissed Henry Jackson as a hardware-crazed militarist beholden to Boeing and other defense contractors in his state tended to forget that it was Jackson who, with other like-minded

Democrats, reestablished human rights as a central concern of U.S. foreign policy, long before Jimmy Carter was visible on the national radar screen. And it was this commitment to human rights that was the foundation of Scoop's anticommunism. As a kid congressman, he had seen the Buchenwald extermination camp in Germany at the end of World War II. So he knew, in his bones and in his heart, what totalitarianism did to people. And it revolted him.

Not for him, then, the backslapping exchanges with the masters of the Gulag in which so many Western businessmen engaged during the "détente" years. Henry Jackson was willing to do business with the Soviet Union—but political business, the business of blunting the course of Soviet power and getting agreement with an aggressor on the rules that should govern international behavior.

Jackson's genius, which was sometimes obscured by his own rhetoric and was almost completely missed by a stereotyping national media, was to understand that the problem of Soviet power and the problem of war and peace were inextricably linked. The full measure of the Soviet threat had to be taken; but one also had to consider that the full armamentarium of responses to that threat was not exclusively military. Neither accommodation to Soviet power nor hysterical lurches into isolationism, but a steady, careful, long-term effort to change the way the Soviet leadership dealt with the world (which likely meant a fundamental change in how the USSR was governed)—that was the Jackson perspective and perception. It was thoroughly vindicated by the European communist crack-up Scoop did not live to see, but in which he would have reveled.

Scoop Jackson's death also marked the end of an era in Congress. One of Jackson's aides remarked, some months after Scoop died, that he had never before realized the crucial function Jackson served until he watched the Senate without him. Post-Scoop, the ship not only seemed to lack a rudder: the ship lacked ballast. For Henry M. Jackson was the ballast of the Senate when the debate turned to America's role in world affairs. Combining, in his unique way, Roman *gravitas* and Norwegian stolidness, Scoop Jackson kept things honest by setting the boundaries of reasonable discussion on national security issues. As long as Jackson was there, things couldn't get completely out of hand. He was the one figure who could, figuratively, close the door and say to ninety-nine other colleagues of considerable ego,

"Enough is enough. Let's get serious." And in that respect, Jackson has never been replaced. He was the Senate's last adult.

In a book of essays published some years after his death, Charles Horner got the essence of the man and the public servant as well as anyone ever did:

> For as much as Jackson later came to be termed by some "conservative" in his outlook, he was in fact steeped in the progressivism of the Pacific Northwest (James Farley did, after all, once refer to "the 47 states and the soviet of Washington") and its particular notion that law was for the weak—weak individuals and weak nations. Indeed, the idea that law exists to restrain the strong and protect the rights of the weak was at the core of everything Jackson did in the arena of international human rights. As a young prosecutor, Jackson gained a reputation as a tough anti-fascist; as a veteran senator, he seemed just as determined that international law in the grandest sense also serve as the protector of individual liberties. In this respect, there was a line which connected the humblest county ordinance to the loftiest of United Nations pronouncements. The elaboration of the argument might become ever more sophisticated, but the living, breathing, individual human being was always the focus.

There are hedgehogs, and then there are foxes. Democracies are in peril without the former: men and women of steadfast principle. Scoop Jackson was such a man, and American democracy was impoverished at his death.

A Modern Martyr
Franz Jägerstätter (1907–1943)

"Courage," wrote John F. Kennedy while profiling it, is "that most admirable of human virtues. To be courageous requires no exceptional qualifications, no magic formula, no special combination of time, place, and circumstance. It is an opportunity that sooner or later is presented to us all."

Courage and the spiritual life are closely related, for courage is one of the four cardinal virtues, along with prudence, moderation, and justice. In the late Roman Empire, faith required courage, for martyrdom was an ever-present possibility. In an age of increasingly aggressive secularism like our own, in which appeals to "tolerance" often mask a deep intolerance of religious and moral truth, faith requires the courage to be distinctive, to stand out, to cherish the virtues of authentic humanism while affirming that they find their fullness when they're deepened and strengthened by grace. But in either age, courage and the spiritual life are linked because of the consequences of belief. The courage of faith is not only in saying *Credo in unum Deum*; it is even more in embracing the implications of that act of confession and commitment.

Advent, the Church's preparation time for Christmas, is a particularly appropriate time to think about courage and faith, for the Scriptures of Advent are full of courageous people who lived to the full the consequences of their confession of belief: Mary and Joseph, Zechariah and Elizabeth, John the Baptizer, the shepherds and Magi. Advent thus invites us to explore the many dimensions of spiritual courage as they appear in authentic human lives. And that includes lives from our own epoch, whose witness often evokes biblical archetypes.

Franz Jägerstätter was, to all appearances, a most unlikely candidate for martyrdom. An illegitimate child, his father was killed in World War I. As a young man in the obscure Austrian village of

St. Radegund, Jägerstätter was something of a hellion, once arrested for leading a brawl between teenage gangs; the owner of the town's first motorcycle, he was a hearty fellow out for a good time, not someone you would quickly think of if you were asked to name the village's spiritual leading lights. But marriage to a devoutly Catholic woman led him into an intense study of the Bible and the lives of the saints—and into a robust Catholicism that may have surprised those who knew him in his devil-may-care days.

He was the only person in his village to vote against the *Anschluss*, the legal drapery behind which Adolf Hitler absorbed Austria into the Third Reich. And virtually alone among lay Austrian Catholics, Franz Jägerstätter refused to submit to military service in the Wehrmacht. Nazism was to him a false religion, Hitler was an antichrist, and Nazi wars of aggression could in no way be justified under the standards established by Catholicism's just-war tradition. Refused support by his bishop, who wrote that "those who preferred to die in concentration camps rather than bear arms were of innocently erroneous conscience ... cases more to be marveled at than copied", Jägerstätter was taken from his wife and three children (the eldest daughter was not yet six), tried by military court, and beheaded in Berlin on August 9, 1943.

Franz Jägerstätter was no neurotic rebel, searching for a cause in which to be immolated; on the contrary, he was a happily married husband and father with a great deal to live for. Offered noncombatant opportunities by the military court, Jägerstätter refused even that compromise with conscience. Under no circumstances would he burn incense at the altar of the Nazi idol. Abandoned by his Church, he died very much alone.

Issues of war, peace, and personal responsibility are not easily resolved. Participation in war involves one kind of moral price; refusal to participate can involve another moral price, especially if an aggressor doesn't share your moral sensibilities. Yet what Franz Jägerstätter so intensely symbolizes is the need to make up one's mind—to face the terrible dilemmas of faith's consequences with serious purpose rather than to dissolve them away into the kinds of petty compromises that often mark (and mar) the spiritual life.

Like William Howard Taft in Theodore Roosevelt's devastating characterization, Christians for whom the faith is merely a lifestyle choice "mean well feebly". Franz Jägerstätter was beatified in 2007 by a German pope, Benedict XVI, after the promoters of his cause finally overcame decades of resistance from Austrian churchmen. His life and death stand in witness to the fact that purposefulness and conviction are still possibilities.

If we have the courage to grasp them.

Conviction Changing History
Pope Saint John Paul II (1920–2005)

He once described his high school years as a time in which he was "completely absorbed" by a passion for the theater. So it was fitting that Karol Józef Wojtyła lived a very dramatic life. As a young man, he risked summary execution by leading clandestine acts of cultural resistance to the Nazi occupation of Poland. As a fledgling priest, he adopted a Stalin-era nom de guerre—*Wujek* (uncle)—while creating zones of intellectual and spiritual freedom for college students; those students, many of whom became distinguished professionals, called him *Wujek* to the end. As archbishop of Kraków, he successfully fought the attempt by Poland's communist overseers to erase the nation's cultural memory. As the first Slavic pope in history, he came home to Poland in June 1979 and over nine days, during which the history of the twentieth century pivoted, he ignited a revolution of conscience that helped make possible the collapse of European communism a decade later.

At his death and during the week of mourning that followed, the world remembered the drama of this life, even as it measured John Paul II's many other accomplishments: his transformation of the papacy from a primarily managerial office to one of evangelical witness; his voluminous teaching, touching virtually every aspect of contemporary life; his dogged pursuit of Christian unity; his success in blocking the Clinton administration's efforts to have abortion-on-demand declared a basic human right; his remarkable magnetism for young people; his groundbreaking initiatives with Judaism; his robust defense of religious freedom as the first of human rights.

And, in that remembering, certain unforgettable images came to mind: the young Pope bouncing infants in the air and the old Pope bowed in remembrance over the memorial flame at Yad Vashem, Jerusalem's Holocaust memorial; the Pope wearing a Kenyan tribal chieftain's feathered crown; the Pope waving his papal cross in defiance of Sandinista demonstrators in Managua; the Pope skiing; the Pope lost in prayer in countless venues; the Pope kneeling at the grave of murdered Solidarity chaplain Jerzy Popiełuszko; the Pope slumped in pain in the popemobile, seconds after being hit by shots from a Browning 9 mm semi-automatic—and the Pope counseling and encouraging the would-be assassin in his Roman prison cell.

During his life and after his death, some dismissed him as hopelessly "conservative" in matters of doctrine and morals, although it is not clear how religious and moral truth can be parsed in liberal/conservative terms, or how a man who devoted much of his intellectual life to exploring the frontiers of contemporary philosophy could be "conservative". The shadows cast upon his papacy by clerical scandal and the misgovernance of some bishops focused others' attention. John Paul II was the most visible human being in history, having been seen live by more men and women than any other man who ever lived; the remarkable thing is that millions of those people, most of whom saw him only at a great distance, thought at his death that they had lost a friend. Those who knew him more intimately experienced a profound sense of personal loss at the death of a man who was so wonderfully, thoroughly, engagingly human—a man of intelligence and wit and courage whose humanity breathed integrity and sanctity.

So there were and are many ways of remembering and mourning him. Pope John Paul II should also be remembered, however, as a man with a penetrating insight into the currents that flow beneath the surface of history, currents that in fact create history, often in surprising ways.

In a 1968 letter to the French Jesuit theologian Henri de Lubac, then-Cardinal Karol Wojtyła suggested that "a kind of degradation, indeed a pulverization, of the fundamental uniqueness of each human person" was at the root of the twentieth century's grim record: two World Wars, Auschwitz and the Gulag, a Cold War threatening global disaster, oceans of blood and mountains of corpses. How had a century begun with such high hopes for the human future produced mankind's greatest catastrophes? Because, Karol Wojtyła proposed, Western humanism had gone off the rails, collapsing into forms of self-absorption, and then self-doubt, so severe that men and women had begun to wonder whether there was any truth to be found in the world—or in themselves.

This profound crisis of culture, this crisis in the very idea of the human, had manifested itself in the serial crises that had marched across the surface of contemporary history, leaving carnage in their wake. But unlike some truly "conservative" critics of late modernity, Wojtyła's counterproposal was not rollback; rather, it was a truer, nobler humanism, built on the foundation of the biblical conviction that God had made the human creature in his image and likeness, with intelligence and free will, a creature capable of knowing the good and freely choosing it. That, John Paul II insisted in a vast number of variations on one great theme, was the true measure of man—the human capacity, in cooperation with God's grace, for heroic virtue.

Here was an idea with consequences, and the Pope applied it to effect across a broad spectrum of issues.

One variant form of debased humanism was the notion that "history" is driven by the politics of willfulness (the Jacobin heresy) or by economics (the Marxist heresy). During his epic pilgrimage to Poland in June 1979, at a moment when "history" seemed frozen and Europe permanently divided into hostile camps, John Paul II demonstrated that "history" worked differently, because human beings aren't just the byproducts of politics or economics. He gave back to his people their authentic history and culture—their identity—and in doing so, he gave them tools of resistance that communist truncheons, water guns, and bullets could not match. Fourteen months after teaching that great lesson in dignity, the Pope watched and guided the emergence of Solidarity, the "independent, self-governing trade union" that became a massive movement of national self-renewal. And then the entire world began to see the communist tide recede, like the slow retreat of a plague.

After the Cold War, when more than a few analysts and politicians were in a state of barely restrained euphoria, imagining a golden age of inevitable progress for the cause of political and economic freedom, John Paul II saw more deeply and clearly. He quickly decoded new threats to what he had called, in that 1968 letter to Father de Lubac, the "inviolable mystery of the human person", and so he spent much of the 1990s explaining that freedom untethered from moral truth risks self-destruction.

For if there is only your truth and my truth and neither one of us recognizes a transcendent moral standard (call it "the truth") by which to settle our differences, then either you will impose your power on me or I will impose my power on you; Nietzsche, great, mad prophet of the twentieth century, got at least that right. Freedom uncoupled from truth, John Paul taught, leads to chaos and thence to new forms of tyranny. For, in the face of chaos (or fear), raw power will inexorably replace persuasion, compromise, and agreement as the coin of the political realm. The false humanism of freedom misconstrued as "I did it my way" inevitably leads to freedom's decay, and then to freedom's self-cannibalization. This was not the soured warning of an antimodern scold; this was the sage counsel of a man who had given his life to freedom's cause from 1939 on.

Thus the key to the freedom project in the twenty-first century, John Paul urged, lay in the realm of culture: in vibrant public moral cultures capable of disciplining and directing the tremendous energies— economic, political, aesthetic, and, yes, sexual—set loose in free societies. A vibrant public moral culture is essential for democracy and the market, for only such a culture can inculcate and affirm the virtues necessary to make freedom work. Democracy and the free economy, he taught in his 1991 encyclical *Centesimus Annus*, are goods; but they are not machines that can blithely run by themselves. Building the free society certainly involves getting the institutions right; beyond that, however, freedom's future depends on men and women of virtue, capable of knowing and choosing the good, and committed to living in solidarity with others.

That is why John Paul relentlessly preached genuine tolerance— not the tolerance of indifference, as if differences over the good didn't matter, but the real tolerance of differences engaged, explored, and debated within the bond of a profound respect for the humanity of the other. Many were puzzled that this Pope, so vigorous in defending the truths of Catholic faith, could become, over a quarter-century, the world's premier icon of religious freedom and interreligious civility. But here, too, John Paul II was teaching a crucial lesson about the future of freedom: universal empathy comes through, not around, particular convictions. Political philosopher John Rawls was wrong. There is no veil of ignorance behind which the world can withdraw, to emerge subsequently with decency in its pocket.

There is only history. But that history, the Pope believed, is the story of God's quest for us, and men and women freely taking the same path as God. "History" is His-story. Believing that, Karol Józef Wojtyła, Pope John Paul II, changed history. The power of his belief empowered millions of others to do the same.

The Broadness of a Gauge
Pope Saint John Paul II (1920–2005)

All lives run along a set of rails: family background, native abilities, education, interests and habits. Karol Wojtyła, Pope John Paul II, was a man whose life ran along a particularly broad-gauged rail bed. He was the most visible human being in history, yet he had a deeply ingrained sense of privacy and an old-fashioned, even courtly, sense of manners. He inspired tens of millions of people by the intensity of his faith; yet he was a mystic who found it impossible to describe some of his own most profound religious experiences. He was arguably the most well-informed man of his time; yet he rarely read newspapers. He had a profound impact on the late twentieth century; yet he was completely convinced that culture, not politics or economics, was the engine that drove history. He had a deep appreciation of untutored popular piety; yet he was a world-class intellectual insatiably curious about the latest trends in philosophy and literature.

The rhythm of his life was prayer. The best hour of his day was the hour of private devotion and meditation in his chapel before his morning Mass. There visitors could hear him groaning in prayer, in a conversation with God that was, quite literally, beyond words. In addition to Mass and the Divine Office, he could be heard in prayer walking back and forth to meetings, taking a stroll in the Vatican gardens, or relaxing after lunch in the garden atop the Apostolic Palace in the Vatican, where he lived.

Breaking centuries of institutionalized habit, he insisted on being the master of his own table, inviting guests for lunch and dinner virtually every day of his pontificate. In numerous mealtime encounters with him over a decade, I discovered Wojtyła to be a remarkably unaffected and natural man, with a capacity to put even the most reticent visitors, men and women, laity and clergy, at ease. He seemed to care little about food, but he had a serious sweet tooth; in his later years he drank herbal tea while his guests were served good local wines with plainly cooked pasta, roast chicken or thinly sliced veal, and a large array of vegetables. Conversation, not carbohydrates, was the sustenance he most craved.

His table talk was often conducted in three or four languages simultaneously. He was the most intense listener I have ever met, a man far more interested in what you had to say than in telling you what he thought—or, still less, what to think. In the space of a half-hour he could guide a conversation from world politics to the goings-on in a guest's parish church, from inquiries about intellectuals whose careers he followed to questions about a visitor's children. His memory for names was phenomenal, and he could startle you by recounting entire conversations you had had with him years before.

His sense of humor was robust and dry. Having no use for sycophants, he liked to kid and he liked to be kidded. His sense of humor about his own life and circumstances tended toward the ironic. Once, after his less than successful 1994 hip-replacement surgery, I asked him how he felt. "Neck down, not so good" was the wry reply. After dinner one night at the papal summer residence at Castel Gandolfo, his secretary brought a raft of documents that required his signature; some of them, to Emperor this or President that, were inscribed on parchment in a beautiful Latin calligraphy. Halfway through the pile he looked across the table at me, obviously tired after a long day, and with raised eyebrow said, *"Povero papa!"*—"The poor pope!" He broke up laughing, and so did the rest of us at the table.

During the three and a half years I was in regular conversation with John Paul II while writing the first volume of his biography, I was struck by the intensity of his friendships and by their endurance. Once you were Wojtyła's friend, you were his friend for life, and he worked hard to keep his friendships green. He also shared his friends with others, encouraging me, for example, to dig into the relationships with young lay men and women that he had formed in the 1950s and that had decisively shaped his vision of the priesthood. Other popes, asked about their earliest priestly experiences, would have talked about their first days teaching in a seminary or their years at the *Accademia*, the exclusive Roman school for the Vatican's diplomats. John Paul II talked about his lay friends in Kraków, their treks into the mountains south of the city, or their kayaking trips along Poland's rivers. It was a telling difference.

In an age in which personalities are often assembled from bits and pieces of conviction (politics here, religion there; morals from here, artistic interests from there), Wojtyła could be startling. He was an extraordinarily integrated personality, and everything about him revolved around the conviction that Jesus Christ is the answer to the question that is every human life. Whether he was meeting Mikhail Gorbachev or the Union of Italian Hairdressers, the children of friends or the princes of his own church, every encounter took place within the horizon of John Paul II's absolutely unshakable conviction that the men and women he met were players in a great cosmic drama that had God as its author and director.

By the conventions of his time, the intensity of his Christian conviction should have made him a sectarian, even a dangerous man. To his mind, however, it was precisely his Christian faith and his discipleship that required him to be in dialogue with everyone. Everyone was of inestimable value, and everything was of interest, because God had entered history in Jesus of Nazareth, supercharging the world and humanity with a grandeur beyond imagining.

"In the designs of Providence there are no mere coincidences," he said in 1982, on the first anniversary of the assassination attempt that came within millimeters of ending his life in a pool of blood on the floor of the popemobile. For Wojtyła, that was *the* truth of the world. Acting on that truth, he became both an immensely attractive human being and one of the great shapers of contemporary history. At his death, those who knew him understood that this world traveler was, finally, where he had always wanted to be.

The Negotiator

Max Kampelman (1920–2013)

In early 1990, Ambassador Max Kampelman—former nuclear arms reduction negotiator with the Soviet Union and Counselor to the Department of State—decided that I needed a bit of diplomatic experience and invited me to be a public member of the U.S. delegation he would lead to the Copenhagen meeting of the Conference on Security and Cooperation in Europe, in the summer of that year.

It was an interesting gathering, being the first review of the "Helsinki Accords" since the Berlin Wall had fallen. The head of the Romanian delegation had a noticeable and somewhat ominous bulge beneath the armpit of his jacket. The head of delegation of another country, which had best remain unnamed, wore a three-piece suit that seemed to have been dry-cleaned in vichyssoise. The intellectual leading lights of the just-completed Revolution of 1989—the Czechoslovaks (as they then were) and the Poles—were fully up to speed in their approach to our topic, which was establishing the rule of law in a postcommunist Europe; others, it seemed, would take longer to acclimate themselves to the New (democratic) Order.

My job was to help with the ambassador's speeches and to liaise with the Holy See delegation (which was, in fact, one person). Max and I worked out several sharp, substantive statements that were not feel-good pablum: on the meaning of pluralism (differences engaged civilly, not differences ignored); on the priority of religious freedom in any meaningful scheme of human rights; on the moral (not merely pragmatic) superiority of the rule of law to sheer coercion. I also learned how to sit placidly, feigning interest, to remarkably long-winded speeches from professional gabblers, in the days before you could plug your iPhone into your simultaneous translation earphones and thus enjoy some serious music while the diplomatese, like Ol' Man River, just kept rollin' along.

On the last day, Max gave me lunch and asked me what I had learned. "A great reverence for my great-grandfather's widowed mother," I replied. The ambassador's puzzlement invited further explanation: "... who had the sense to get out of this patchwork of quarreling tribes and come to America." Max's own parents being émigré Romanian Jews, he was not inclined to contest my point.

Prior to his death at ninety-two on January 25, 2013, Max Kampelman could look back on a lifetime of high adventure and great achievement. He was a World War II conscientious objector who nevertheless contributed to the nation's war effort by volunteering for a starvation experiment at the University of Minnesota that dropped him to one hundred pounds but taught medical lessons that saved the lives of former POWs and death-camp survivors. He took advanced degrees in both law and political science and became a *consigliere* to Hubert Humphrey, whom he might well have served as White House counsel had the 1968 election gone differently.

He was a major figure in forcing human rights issues onto the U.S. foreign policy agenda, made an invaluable contribution to the moral delegitimation of the Soviet Union as ambassador for Presidents Carter and Reagan to the Madrid Review Conference on the Helsinki Accords in the early 1980s, and then worked himself into a heart attack negotiating a nuclear arms reduction pact with the USSR. In his last years, Max joined forces with other foreign policy heavyweights like Henry Kissinger, George Shultz, and Sam Nunn in urging that the elimination of nuclear weapons become a national policy goal.

Throughout his public life, Max, who was not an especially pious man, worked out of the Jewish moral heritage he cherished: there was good in men and women, and it should be encouraged; there was evil in people and in the world, and it must be fought; true political authority had to serve the cause of justice.

When Max helped arrange my 1983–1984 fellowship at the Woodrow Wilson International Center for Scholars and thus my relocation to Washington, D.C., neither one of us thought he was incubating a papal biographer. But as his life had taken surprising turns, so did mine, not without his help. The point, he would insist, was to live vocationally.

The Lutheran Catholic Pastor
Leonard Klein (1945–2019)

In January 2009, the vigil service and funeral Mass for Father Richard John Neuhaus were held at the parish he had served, the Church of the Immaculate Conception in the Gramercy Flatiron neighborhood of Manhattan. Some may have imagined that Neuhaus, a prominent New York figure for decades, would be buried from St. Patrick's Cathedral, as his great friend, Cardinal Avery Dulles, S.J., had been, a month earlier. But the Archdiocese of New York was not enthusiastic about that idea. And in any event Father Neuhaus had made it quite clear before his death that he wanted his wake and funeral Mass to be celebrated among the working class people to whom he had preached in his singular way—never talking down, but always lifting up.

The unsettled question was, who would preside at the vigil service? Father Neuhaus' old friend Robert Louis Wilken and I believed that the vigil should reflect Neuhaus' Lutheran heritage. So with the concurrence of Neuhaus' devoutly Lutheran sisters we invited Father Leonard Klein to celebrate the vigil service. Father Klein did a masterful job of leading a packed church (and those standing outside on 14th Street) in prayer. His homily, however, caused more than a few parishioners' jaws to drop when he casually mentioned that he and his wife, Christa, had first met in the basement of then–Pastor Neuhaus' Lutheran church in the then-tough Bedford-Stuyvesant section of Brooklyn. The largely Filipino locals were puzzled: Isn't this guy a *priest*? What's this business about his *wife*?

Like his old friend Neuhaus, Leonard Klein was a longtime Lutheran pastor who, unable to preach and minister any longer within the doctrinal and moral confusions of the Evangelical Lutheran Church in America [ELCA], entered into full communion with the Catholic Church in 2003. The former Pastor Klein then sought permission from the Holy See to be ordained to the priesthood as a married man.

Permission was granted, and Leonard was duly ordained by Bishop Michael Saltarelli of Wilmington in 2006, with Christa and their children in attendance.

My small role in the ecumenical drama of this exceptionally good man's life was a partial repayment on a large debt (to which I'll avert in a moment). Leonard had called me in 2002 from his church in York, Pennsylvania, saying that we needed to talk. I had a hunch what was coming and, sure enough, over a conversation at St. Mary's Seminary and University in Baltimore (where Dr. Christa Klein was then running the institute for continuing clergy education), Leonard told me that it was impossible in conscience for him to remain in ELCA any longer. After thanking him for his honesty and courage, I asked whether he hoped to continue in the active ministry as a Catholic. He did. Then I asked whether he'd discussed the matter with Cardinal William Keeler, the archbishop of Baltimore. He had. But Keeler had just accepted two married Episcopalian clergy into full communion; both men were candidates for the priesthood under the "Pastoral Provision"; and the cardinal, ever cautious, thought that that was about all the traffic could bear. I then suggested the possibility of Leonard's being ordained for the Diocese of Wilmington, near the Klein's Pennsylvania home, and said I'd make an inquiry. A few hours later, I called Monsignor John Barres (later the bishop of Rockville Centre), who was serving as chancellor of the diocese for Wilmington's Bishop Saltarelli, and opened the conversation by saying, "Have I got an early Christmas present for you!"

Leonard Klein was indeed an extraordinary gift to the Catholic Church in Wilmington; but he was the giver of the gift (which he would insist was a matter of God's grace working through him). In Wilmington, he first served as a member of the diocesan Family Life Bureau and as a hospital chaplain before becoming pastor of two parishes and ultimately rector of the Cathedral of St. Peter (while concurrently serving as pastor of yet two other parishes). To all of those assignments, as to his pro-life work and his chaplaincy to the diocesan St. Thomas More Society, he brought a gentlemanly mien, a profound faith, a deep biblical sensibility, a crisp theological intelligence—and that gift for expository preaching that many Catholics wish their priests would learn from their Lutheran colleagues in

Christian ministry. Born in 1945, and thus a half-generation behind Richard Neuhaus and Robert Wilken in his theological formation, Leonard was nonetheless, and like them, influenced by Arthur Carl Piepkorn, longtime professor of systematic theology at Concordia Seminary, St. Louis, who taught men like Neuhaus, Wilken, and Klein that Lutheranism should understand itself as a reforming movement within the one, holy, catholic, and apostolic Church, not as one among many Protestant denominations.

That was, and is, a minority view in Lutheran circles. But Piepkorn's perspective was an exceptionally fruitful one. For it inspired many Lutheran pastors who, whether they eventually entered into full communion with the Catholic Church or not, helped bridge a centuries-old ecumenical chasm; at the same time, they kept alive a tradition of confessional Lutheranism that was absolutely serious about the authority of the Scriptures and the ancient creeds of the Church. Catholics could only benefit from contact with these pastors, as I certainly did. And one expression of my gratitude for what I had learned from men like Neuhaus and Wilken was to do my small bit to help Leonard Klein find a ministerial home in the Catholic Church.

Leonard and Christa Klein lived a great Christian marriage, and Christa's exquisite care for Leonard during his last illness—a heroic battle against leukemia that lasted a long time and involved no little physical suffering from the aftereffects of a bone-marrow transplant—helped everyone who loved this extraordinary Christian couple deepen their understanding of a one-flesh union in Christ and how it can be, as Saint Paul taught his Ephesians, an icon of the love of Christ for his bride, the Church (5:21–33).

Like others in their distinctive situation whom I've been privileged to know, Leonard and Christa Klein understood and cherished celibacy as the normative tradition in the Latin-Rite Church's priesthood and were skeptical of progressive Catholicism's enthusiasm for abandoning that venerable practice. It was Christa Klein, for example, who described for me the pressures that a wife feels when married to a Catholic priest (who is, in a very real sense, "married" to his local Church and bishop). And it was Christa who then wondered aloud why so few Catholic campaigners for optional celibacy ever considered how this would affect marriages from the wife's point of view. Her own extensive work with clergy formation in both Protestant and Catholic seminary contexts gave, and will continue to give, Christa Klein a special wisdom and authority in these discussions.

During the pontificates of John Paul II and Benedict XVI, it was not all that uncommon for confessionally serious and theologically astute Lutheran, Presbyterian, and Anglican clergy to seek full communion with the Catholic Church, which they saw as a bulwark against the acid effects on ecclesial life of the theological liberalism deplored by the greatest of modern converts, Saint John Henry Newman. That stream of "crossover" clergy seems to have run somewhat dry under Pope Francis. And while there are doubtless many reasons for that, including generational differences, the sense in some quarters that the Catholic Church in the third decade of the twenty-first century was in some danger of losing its grip on its doctrinal and moral identity, and thus on its doctrinal and moral boundaries, was surely part of the picture.

There will be time enough to consider that. It is enough, now, to give thanks for the life and ministry of Father Leonard Klein, who as both Lutheran pastor and Catholic priest was a shining witness to what it means to be a good shepherd of the flock. He nourished his people with the Word of God and the grace of the sacraments; he could do so because he was himself a radically converted Christian whose ministry grew out of a life of prayer and study. Leonard Klein's distinctive life experience is not easily replicable. But his example, as a Christian and a minister of the Gospel, could well be emulated by many.

The Great Pathologist of the Most Lethal Heresy
Leszek Kołakowski (1927–2009)

Leszek Kołakowski will be remembered by the world of letters as one of the leading philosophers of the late twentieth century, a man whose magisterial *Main Currents of Marxism* will be read centuries from now by anyone interested in getting at the intellectual roots of one of modernity's most consequential—and lethal—bodies of thought. His native Poland will remember Kołakowski as one of a small group of intellectuals who, in the aftermath of the Soviet brutalization of Hungary in 1956 and Czechoslovakia in 1968, turned their backs on theoretical Marxism as well as on the Communist Party, wrecking their own academic careers but laying some of the paving stones that would eventually lead to the Solidarity movement, the nonviolent collapse of European communism, and the triumph of freedom in much of Central and Eastern Europe.

Those memories will be true to the man and his accomplishment. But when I think of Leszek Kołakowski, the first thing that comes to mind is perhaps the worst dive I've ever been in: the hard-currency bar in the basement of the Europa, a "five-star" Moscow hotel, in October 1990.

I was in the Soviet capital with a group of political thinkers and writers, most of them American, meeting for a week with men and women who thought of themselves as the democratic opposition to Mikhail Gorbachev—whom none of our Russian interlocutors imagined to be much of a democrat. It was a week of bad food, intense conversation about the legal and cultural building blocks of democracy, irritating surveillance by the KGB, and the exhilaration of fomenting a democratic revolution in the belly of the beast. When we first got to our hotel rooms, it was obvious even to amateurs that they were bugged. So my colleagues and I agreed that we would meet occasionally in the hotel's hard-currency bar, admission to which required either U.S. dollars or Deutschmarks, for debriefing and planning. We figured that

the excruciatingly loud rock music—and not very good rock at that—
would forestall eavesdropping on our conversations about that day's
happenings and the next day's plans by any ferrets who happened to
be lurking about.

It was an awful dump, with East German prostitutes standing all
along the perimeter, the air chokingly thick with smoke. The sight
of Leszek Kołakowski in that dive, sitting on a shabby divan and
dispensing wisdom while sipping cherry brandies and politely batting
away the frauleins who tried to plop themselves into his lap, is one I
shall never forget.

Just as unforgettable, though, was the walk I took with Leszek
on a cool morning, before our daily meetings began. A kind of tent
city had been set up at one end of Red Square, full of impoverished country people who had come to Moscow to ask for redress of
their various grievances, many of which were displayed on crudely
fashioned homemade posters. The exquisite sensitivity with which
the great philosophical pathologist of Marxism engaged one after
another of these sad souls—listening carefully, offering words of
encouragement—bespoke a decency and a capacity for human solidarity that was nothing short of inspiring. Indeed, one of those in
whom I sensed similar attributes was another Polish philosopher:
Karol Wojtyła, Pope John Paul II.

Were it the only thing he had ever written, *Main Currents of Marxism*, Kołakowski's three-volume masterwork, would have made him
a worthy first recipient of the Library of Congress' Kluge Prize for
lifetime achievement in the humanities and social sciences. (Leszek's
feisty and brilliant daughter, Agnieszka, told me that Her Majesty's
Inland Revenue had kept a goodly percentage of the cool million
dollars given to awardees by the generous Mr. Kluge.) *Main Currents*,
however, was only one part of Kołakowski's extensive oeuvre, which
combined the kind of rigorous logic for which pre–World War
II Polish philosophy was noted with wit and literary grace. Kołakowski's small book *Why Is There Something Rather Than Nothing?
23 Questions from Great Philosophers* is a gem that ought to be required
reading for every college freshman—for Kołakowski was a brilliant
teacher as well as a gifted writer, a man who forced you to think even
when you disagreed. Then there is *My Correct Views on Everything*,
in which he explains his break with Marxism (while eviscerating the

British Marxist E. P. Thompson, who wrote a notorious "Open Letter to Leszek Kołakowski") and then goes on to explore Christianity and classical liberalism in a brace of finely honed essays. Kołakowski's philosophical works on religion ought to give the New Atheists pause; they, and others, might begin with *Religion: If There Is No God ... On God, the Devil, Sin, and Other Worries of the So-Called Philosophy of Religion* (Leszek did have a way with titles).

But in trying to summarize the achievement of a brilliant and original thinker who endured both political exile and a lot of physical suffering, I still return to those days in Moscow in October 1990—albeit to a scene from which Leszek was absent. Brad Roberts, then the editor of the *Washington Quarterly*, and I decided to spend a few free hours exploring the Kremlin, and we enlisted as guide a bright young Russian who had been hanging around our hotel lobby, obviously looking to practice his English. He took us to one of the newly restored cathedrals inside the Kremlin walls, where we soon found ourselves standing before a cleaned and luminous late-medieval fresco of the Last Supper. There was no doubt that it was the Last Supper; it couldn't have been anything else. Yet this obviously intelligent young Russian looked at us and said, "Please tell me: who are those men and what are they doing?"

That was what seventy years of communism had done to a generation: it had lobotomized them culturally. Leszek Kołakowski's philosophical project was a long, rigorous, deeply humane protest against that kind of spiritual vandalism. Kołakowski knew that European civilization was built on the foundations of biblical religion, Greek philosophy, and Roman law. It was built, that is, on the conviction that life is not just one damn thing after another; a robust confidence in the human capacity to get to the truth of things; and a settled determination to order societies by means other than sheer coercion. Leszek Kołakowski's defense of the civilization of the West against the barbarism he was convinced was inherent in the Marxist enterprise was an impressive intellectual accomplishment. It was also the accomplishment of a noble soul.

Brightening Friday Mornings
Charles Krauthammer (1950–2018)

Take my word for it: You don't want to be around me at breakfast. I am not a chipper morning person, and it's best to leave me to the coffee and the newspapers—and I mean news*papers*, not the online editions—until I become fit for human company. There was, however, an exception to my congenital early morning grumpiness and it involved thirty-two years of Fridays. Because on Friday mornings, for more than three decades, my first semi-conscious thought was, "I wonder what Charles is writing about today?" The answer rarely disappointed.

The encomia that followed Charles Krauthammer's announcement that he was terminally ill, and that continued after his death, were appropriately full of praise for his courage and kindness. In my satchel of Krauthammer memories, my personal favorite may cast some new light on this much-praised man, who made Friday mornings brighter with his weekly column, no matter what the subject on which he wrote.

It was October 18, 1999, a few weeks after the first volume of my John Paul II biography, *Witness to Hope*, was published, and the Ethics and Public Policy Center was hosting a book signing and reception. Things were a lot more civil in the nation's capital in those days, and the party was attended by Democrats and Republicans, conservatives and liberals, politicos and pundits, Catholics, Protestants, Jews, and Nones. I thanked all those who had supported me during the years of preparation that had gone into the book, and then I began signing. The line was considerable and after about a half-hour I was surprised to find Charles approaching my table in his wheelchair, a book he'd just purchased in hand. "Oh, no," I said. "You were on the review copy list; didn't the publisher get you a copy?" "This isn't for me," he replied. "It's for Daniel."

Charles Krauthammer, a man who took intense pride in his Jewish heritage but had a complicated relationship with the God of Jews and Christians, wanted his son to know about Pope John Paul II. In detail. We were seventeen years into our friendship and I thought Charles had run out of ways to surprise me, but I was both surprised and deeply touched.

Everyone has Charles stories, and I'm no exception.

I remember being in his home and watching Russian grandmaster and human rights activist Gary Kasparov play three other chess whizzes at once on the Krauthammer kitchen table in timed matches—if memory serves, the others had thirty seconds to make a move and the great Kasparov had ten. I need not say who won.

I remember going to the last Opening Day at old Memorial Stadium in Baltimore with Charles in 1991 and spending the better part of four hours swapping baseball trivia with another kind of grandmaster.

I remember a seminar on the moral and legal questions of U.S. intervention in world affairs that I helped organize, in which Charles debated, in the most civil way, Father J. Bryan Hehir, the intellectual architect of the U.S. bishops' 1983 letter on war and peace. It was an extraordinarily intelligent exchange of views, and at the end of the seminar, Jim Woolsey, a former Undersecretary of the Navy who would go on to become the director of central intelligence, exhaled with satisfaction and said, "That was major league."

I remember bringing Charles some mementos of my first visit to one of the ancient synagogues of Kraków, where an ancestor of his, whose portrait he kept in his office, had been chief rabbi, hundreds of years before.

And I remember Charles asking, two months after the implosion of the Soviet Union, "What are we going to do with the rest of our lives?" The great struggle in which we'd been comrades had been won; now what? I said that I didn't think history was over, and that there would be a lot for each of us to do.

That was indeed the way things turned out. There was a lot more to do. Charles did it with consummate skill for the next quarter-century. He now rests with the fathers, and I imagine Abraham is pleased to have his company, much as the rest of us miss him. Especially on Friday mornings.

A Blessing for the World
Aaron Jean-Marie Lustiger (1926–2007)

Prior to the catastrophic fire of April 2019, visitors to the Cathedral of Notre-Dame in Paris were able, should they like, to ponder a commemorative marker carrying this inscription:

"I was born Jewish. I received the name of my paternal grandfather, Aaron. Having become Christian by faith and by baptism, I have remained Jewish as did the Apostles. I have as my patron saints Aaron the High Priest, Saint John the Apostle, Holy Mary full of grace. Named 139th archbishop of Paris by His Holiness, Pope John Paul II, I was enthroned in this cathedral on 27 February 1981, and here I exercised my entire ministry. Passers by, pray for me."

In the early 1950s, two young men whose names would become familiar throughout the world attended the same political science lectures at the Sorbonne. One was the son of Polish-Jewish parents; the other came from Cambodia. One had lost his mother in Hitler's Holocaust; the other would ignite a holocaust. One had converted to Catholicism; the other had converted to Marxism. One would live to become the embodiment of humane, intellectually coherent religious faith, and thereby give hope to his people; the other would marry irrationality to viciousness, and his name would become a curse among his people.

One was named Aaron Jean-Marie Lustiger. The other was named Pol Pot. A novelist of sufficient imagination could turn that scene—Lustiger and Pol Pot, in the same Parisian classroom—into a gripping tale about divergent roads taken and the consequences that followed. I'm not a novelist, but I am very grateful for the privilege of having had Jean-Marie Lustiger's life intersect with my own.

We first met in Washington in 1986 or so, when he was visiting America with a group of young aides. After a formal session at the Woodrow Wilson International Center for Scholars, the cardinal and I fell into more informal conversation and I asked him whether this was his first trip to the United States. Oh no, he answered, he had once hitchhiked across the country. "When was that?" I asked. "1968," he replied. I groaned and observed that he might have chosen a more tranquil year.

Cardinal Lustiger was very helpful as I was preparing the first volume of my John Paul II biography, *Witness to Hope*, and we stayed in touch over the years. Early in 2006, one of his assistants, Jean Duchesne, told me that the cardinal, quite ill with cancer, wanted to see me before he died in order to share some memories of, and reflections on, the last years of John Paul II. We spent ninety minutes together in the cardinal's modest Paris apartment in December 2006 and had a conversation that I shall always remember for its Christian lucidity—and for the cardinal's tranquillity in thinking about death in the very face of death. I asked for Lustiger's blessing as I left; I shall always cherish the memory of his hands on my head and his thin arms drawing me into a final embrace. Here was a man of God; here was a man. The first explained the second.

Like John Paul II, Aaron Jean-Marie Lustiger believed that the biblical story—the story that begins with God's self-revelation to the People of Israel and that continues in the Church—is in fact the story of humanity, rightly understood. The biblical story and the human story don't run on parallel tracks; the biblical story *is* the human story, read in its true depth. For Cardinal Lustiger, the "choice of God" (the title of one of his best-selling books) was also the choice for a genuine humanism, the choice for a life without fear of final oblivion—the fear that was one root of the lethally different choice his Cambodian classmate had made.

Cardinal Lustiger, who wrote with great insight about worship and prayer, knew that at the heart of culture is cult. Everyone worships; the question is whether the object of our worship is a worthy one. Having lived and died in the conviction that worship of the God of Abraham, Isaac, Jacob, and Jesus is true worship, Aaron Jean-Marie Lustiger became a blessing for the world.

Papal Bull

Paul V. Mankowski, S.J. (1953–2020)

When the choirs of angels led Father Paul Mankowski, S.J., into the Father's House on September 3, 2020, I hope the seraphic choirmaster chose music appropriate to the occasion. Had I been asked, I would have suggested the Latin antiphon *Ecce sacerdos magnus* as arranged by Anton Bruckner. The all-stops-pulled moments in Bruckner's composition, deploying organ, brass, and full choir, would have been a perfect match for Paul Mankowski's rock-solid Catholic faith, his heroic ministry, and his robust literary and oratorical style. The *a capella* sections, softly sung, mirror the gentleness with which he healed souls. Above all, I would have suggested Bruckner's motet because Father Mankowski truly was what the antiphon celebrates: "a great priest who in his days pleased God".

We were friends for some thirty years, and I can say without reservation that I have never met anyone like Paul Mankowski. He was off-the-charts brilliant, an extraordinary linguist and scholar; but he wore his learning lightly and was a tremendous wit. He rarely expressed doubts about anything; but he displayed a great sensitivity to the doubts and confusions of those who had the humility to confess that they were at sea. He could be as fierce as Jeremiah in denouncing injustice and dishonesty; but the compassion he displayed to spiritually wounded fellow priests and laity, who sought healing through the work of grace at his hands, was just as notable a feature of his personality.

His *curriculum vitae* was singular. The son of working-class parents, he put himself through the University of Chicago working summers in a steel mill. He did advanced degrees at Oxford and Harvard, becoming the sparring partner of a future Australian prime minister, Tony Abbott, at the former, and delving deeply into the mysteries of Semitic philology—unfathomable, to most of his friends—at the latter. He taught biblical Hebrew at the Pontifical Biblical Institute in Rome, tried to teach Latin to rowdy high school students on the west side of Chicago, and was pastor of an English-speaking parish in Amman, Jordan. Wherever he was, he lived like a true ascetic; he was also the best company imaginable at a meal or a party.

He was a writer of genius, although his published bibliography is considerably slimmer than it might have been, thanks to the years when he was silenced or censored by his religious superiors. A good example of his ability to combine keen insight and droll humor is his March 1992 dissection of the goings-on at the annual convention of the American Academy of Religion (published in the March 1992 issue of *First Things*). More recently, Father Mankowski drew on his extensive experience as a confessor and spiritual director to pen, with his superiors' permission, a respectful but sharp critique of his fellow Jesuit James Martin's book *Building a Bridge* (also published in *First Things*, August-September 2017). In the decades between those two pieces, and when permitted to do so, he published essays and reviews on a wide range of topics, including literature, politics, Church affairs, biblical translations, and the priesthood, while sharing his private musings with friends in a seemingly endless series of pungent parodies, revised song lyrics, and imagined news stories.

Years ago, his friend Father Richard John Neuhaus dubbed Father Mankowski one of the "Papal Bulls": Jesuits of a certain generation notable for their intellectually sophisticated and unwavering Catholic orthodoxy, which often got them into hot water of various temperatures (including boiling) with their Ignatian brothers and superiors. Paul Mankowski was no bull, papal or otherwise, in a china shop, though. He relished debate and was courteous in it; what he found off-putting was the unwillingness of Catholic progressives to fight their corner with a frank delineation of their position. This struck him as a form of hypocrisy. And while Father Mankowski, the good shepherd, often brought strays back to the Lord's flock, he was unsparingly candid about what he perceived as intellectual dishonesty, or what he deplored a few months before his untimely death as "ignoble timidity" in facing clerical corruption. Paul Mankowski was not a man of the subjunctive, and he paid the price for it.

He is now beyond all that, and I like to imagine that Saint Ignatius of Loyola welcomed him to the Father's House with a hearty "Well done, my son." In this valley of tears, freshly moistened by all who mourn our loss and the Church's, Father Paul V. Mankowski, S.J., will be remembered by those who loved him as a man and a priest who, remaining faithful to his Jesuit and sacerdotal vocations, became a tower of strength for others. This was a man of God. This was a man whose courageous manliness reflected his godliness.

Number 89
Gino Marchetti (1926–2019)

By the gargantuan standards of the twenty-first-century National Football League, Gino Marchetti, who died on April 29, 2019, was undersized at six foot four and a mere 245 pounds. But he was arguably the greatest pass rusher in pro football history. The official record, twenty-two and a half quarterback "sacks" over sixteen games, was recorded by the New York Giants' Michael Strahan in 2001. But a review of a year's game film by Baltimore Colts' coaches, before the "sack" stat (tackling a quarterback behind the line of scrimmage before he could throw a pass) was officially kept, once disclosed forty-three sacks by Gino in a twelve-game season.

Whatever the record books show, however, Gino Marchetti was a big man in several ways.

His parents were dirt-poor Italian immigrants who made it to America in the days of rigid immigration quotas and set up a bar in Antioch, California. By his own account, Gino, born in 1926, was "a little wild". And after a "certain difficulty" with a high school teacher, he made the prudential judgment that enlisting in the Army was preferable to what awaited him at home: "I figured I could either face the Germans or I could face my father." (Moreover, he discovered to his satisfaction, those who enlisted automatically got their high school diploma.) He made it to Europe in time to fight in the endgame of the Battle of the Bulge and stayed with the Sixty-Ninth Infantry Division as a machine-gunner until V-E Day.

This XL-sized vet with the flowing, jet-back hair then hung around Antioch for a while, riding a Harley in a black leather jacket ("seventeen zippers", he later recalled) and working as a bartender while playing some junior college football. A smart recruiter then asked whether he wanted to play at the University of San Francisco (then both Catholic and Jesuit), and a legend was born.

The 1951 San Francisco Dons were a great team in an era when college football far outstripped the National Football League in fan interest. Ten of those Dons went on to pro careers and three are enshrined in Canton at the Pro Football Hall of Fame. They were unbeaten and untied, but more to the point, they were "uninvited" to a big postseason bowl—not because of a lack of talent but because of an excess of character, a lot of it embodied by Gino Marchetti.

The Dons were wanted by three of the big bowls—Orange, Cotton, and Gator—on condition that they leave their two star black players, Ollie Matson and Burt Toler, back in San Francisco. After their last regular-season game, Coach Joe Kuharik told the team, "We can play in a big Southern bowl game or stay home. It's up to you." Marchetti, according to legend, said, "[Expletive deleted] the big Southern bowl games."

Gino later claimed that all he had said was "No," and that every other white player on the team said the same thing. I prefer the legendary version because it nicely delineates the man's character: morally unambiguous, brave, and loyal, a "man for others" in the parlance of a later generation of universities in the Jesuit tradition. Those same qualities made Gino one of the two centerpieces, along with the immortal John Unitas, of the great Baltimore Colts teams of the late 1950s and early 1960s. That the Colts beat the New York Giants in the first sudden-death championship game in NFL history in 1958 is well-remembered. What's not so well-remembered, except among Baltimore natives of a certain venerability, is that Gino Marchetti was the reason there was a sudden-death overtime.

The Giants were leading late in the fourth quarter when Frank Gifford ran a third-down sweep. Marchetti fought off blockers and stopped Gifford inches short of the first down that would have clinched the game for the New Yorkers. In the pile-up, though, Colts' tackle "Big Daddy" Lipscomb landed on Gino's leg and Marchetti's ankle snapped. "I never hurt so bad in my life," Gino told a reporter. But he insisted on staying on the periphery of the field, lying under a blanket on a stretcher, as the Colts tied the game and sent it into overtime. Their sudden-death win mesmerized the country and firmly embedded the NFL in the nation's sporting consciousness. (In the locker room after the game, a reporter asked whether Marchetti had cried because of the pain in his broken ankle. "I would have," he said, "if I weren't Gino Marchetti.")

Those Colts, like the old Brooklyn Dodgers, experienced their racial tensions. Yet for that era, they, like the Dodgers, modeled teamwork based on the content of a man's character, not his complexion. How did that happen? What made it work, in a segregated city in an era of segregation?

What held them together, African American and Hall of Fame halfback Lenny Moore said years later, was "something inside Gino Marchetti".

R.I.P., Number 89.

A Good Man in a Tough Business
John R. Miller (1938–2017)

In September 2013, after speaking in the Lithuanian Parliament in Vilnius on the twentieth anniversary of Pope John Paul II's visit to that small Baltic country, I ran into three epic figures from the Catholic resistance movement that styled itself the "Lithuanian Catholic Committee for the Defense of Believers' Rights". When I first learned their names, back in the early 1980s, Sigitas Tamkevičius, Alfonsas Svarinskas, and Nijolė Sadūnaitė—a clandestine Jesuit, a diocesan priest, and an underground nun—were all doing hard time in Siberian Gulag camps. Our meeting was a happy one and brought to mind a friend who was a singular figure in contemporary American public life, John R. Miller, who died on October 4, 2017, at the age of seventy-nine— the Jewish congressman from hypersecular Seattle who helped pry Lithuanian Catholic priests and nuns out of the clutches of a crumbling Soviet empire, and later became an advocate for the victims of the twenty-first-century's contribution to the tawdry history of slavery: sex-trafficked girls and women.

An Army veteran and a graduate of Bucknell and the Yale Law School, John Miller had enjoyed a successful career as a Seattle city councilman and television commentator before winning Washington State's First Congressional District seat in 1984. (On the council, Miller was one of those instrumental in saving Seattle's Pike Place Market, so when you next down a Pike Place Roast latte at your local Starbucks, think kindly on his memory.) When he came to Congress in January 1985, my old friend Miller asked me if I would do some part-time consulting work in his congressional office, as I had done for his predecessor in that seat, Joel Pritchard. Like most freshmen in the House minority, John had gotten some decidedly unsexy committee assignments. But irrespective of his committees, he wanted to use his time in Congress to work on his human-rights interests, which were an expression of both his fundamental human

decency and his principled anticommunism—the latter not being a
trait typical of Seattle-area politicos in the post–Scoop Jackson era, or
indeed in that era's latter phase.

When I was first getting to know Miller in Seattle in the late 1970s,
we had both come to the view that human-rights pressure on the
USSR was a key to winning the Cold War. And now, despite his
lowly status among 435 House members, Miller wanted to do something about that. I suggested that he take up a cause that no one else
found very interesting—the cause of Lithuania's persecuted Catholic
human-rights and pro-democracy activists. The six hundredth anniversary of Lithuania's conversion to Christianity was on the horizon
in 1987, and that seemed a good hook on which to hang our work.
So, after finding a congenial Democrat whose district included a significant population of Lithuanian Americans (and whose staff included
a then-obscure young Democratic activist named George Stepha-
nopoulos), Miller and I set about creating the Lithuanian Catholic
Religious Freedom Caucus in the U.S. House of Representatives.

The caucus did the usual things—lobbying the State Department
and the White House, passing resolutions, sponsoring a rally in honor
of that six hundredth anniversary, which was broadcast into Lithuania
on Radio Free Europe and Radio Liberty—and we were eventually successful in helping get Father Tamkevičius (who would later
become Archbishop Tamkevičius of Kaunas and a cardinal), Father
Svarinskas, and Sister Nijolė out of Perm Camp 36 and similar Gulag
stations before Lithuania auto-liberated from the USSR in 1990–1991.

John Miller had no sectarian or denominational interest in Lithuanian Catholicism, but he intuitively understood that these were good
and brave people who deserved support. And while the Lithuanian
Catholic Religious Freedom Caucus won Miller no votes back in
Seattle (the city where one finds, today, a sixteen-foot-tall statue of
Lenin in the Fremont neighborhood), it seemed to John the right
thing to do. So he did it.

That same commitment to the fundamental human decencies also
inspired Miller's work between 2002 and 2006 as ambassador-at-
large and director of the State Department's Office to Monitor and
Combat Trafficking in Persons—a bureaucratic title that does little to
communicate the squalor and horror of the crimes that the office was
meant to prevent or mitigate.

John Miller wore himself out, physically and emotionally, traveling to such hellholes as the slums of Bangkok, where young girls and women were kidnapped or otherwise trapped into the global sex trade, talking to the victims, and learning how such atrocities could happen today. As we met during those years, I could see the toll being taken on this essentially gentle man by his constant immersion in awfulness—and by the frustrations he experienced with European governments such as that of the Netherlands, which needed "sex workers" for its legalized prostitution "industry", and who weren't much interested in the human rights of those "workers". The State Department itself wasn't all that passionate about the problem, not least because it caused friction with allies. So Miller found himself fighting on three fronts: against the traffickers and those who abetted them in Third World countries; against Euro-governments whose concern for "human rights" stopped where the rights in question were those of ten-year-old Thai girls; and against his own government, which too often couldn't be bothered.

Miller resigned his ambassadorship in 2006. And while he doubtless took a bit of satisfaction from what he'd been able to accomplish in putting modest brakes on some trafficking, he was more frustrated and appalled than satisfied. There is still no effective global abolitionist movement against sex trafficking, the twenty-first-century equivalent of the slave trade. But if one ever emerges and wins the day, John Miller will be remembered as a kind of proto–William Wilberforce: the man of moral conviction who refused to accept that to which others chose to turn a blind eye.

After teaching stints at his alma mater in New Haven and at George Washington University, John Miller retired to California, where he penned a novel on what he regarded as an underappreciated but critical moment in American history: George Washington's refusal to let himself be seduced into a military cabal to take over the conduct of national affairs from the inept Continental Congress. *The Man Who Could Be King* was a labor of love, many years in the making. And as things turned out when the cancer he had long battled finally took the upper hand, it was John Miller's farewell love song to the United States.

He was a patriot, an accomplished public servant, and great good company (not least at a baseball game). But above all, John Ripin

Miller was a good and decent man, indelibly marked with a Jewish passion for justice, remembered with affection and esteem by those privileged to know him—and remembered with honor and gratitude by those he tried to liberate from various forms of slavery.

The Great Catholic "What If?"
Daniel Patrick Moynihan (1927–2003)

The 2010 publication of *Daniel Patrick Moynihan: A Portrait in Letters of an American Visionary* was cause for both celebration and sadness: celebration, because his letters reintroduced the country to Pat Moynihan's scintillating intellect, sparkling wit, and penetrating insight into some of the great issues of the late twentieth century; sadness, because Pat was, in his time, the great Catholic "what if ....?" of American public life.

Following, and slightly modifying, the biblical injunction in Sirach 44:1, "Let us [first] praise famous men."

Daniel Patrick Moynihan was one of the five or ten most influential public intellectuals of the second half of the twentieth century, a man whose ideas eventually worked themselves into the hard soil of public policy and then into the texture of American public life. He was among the first to recognize the enduring influence of ethnicity in the political and cultural Mixmaster of modern America, as he was one of the first to identify and empirically describe the social pathologies destroying the African American family—and he was pilloried as a racist for both insights. When most of the Democratic Party went into a post-McGovern swoon of appeasement and neo-isolationism, Pat helped lead the charge for a robust U.S. foreign policy focused on the defeat of communism through the defense of human rights. Long before welfare reform came onto the national radar screen, Moynihan knew that something was desperately wrong with our social services and coined the pellucid phrase "defining deviancy down" to describe the wishful thinking and counterproductive welfare policies then destroying lives, families, and neighborhoods.

And along the way, he became the only man in our history to serve in the cabinet or subcabinet of four consecutive presidents of two different parties: John F. Kennedy, Lyndon B. Johnson, Richard Nixon, and Gerald Ford.

That public service, which led to his 1976 election to the first of four terms in the United States Senate, representing the state of New York, was marked by a rapier-like wit and a bracing, combative public presence. As U.S. ambassador to the United Nations in the mid-1970s, Pat Moynihan raised polemics to a new art form while flagellating various corrupters of the moral coin of international public life; his speech condemning the General Assembly's infamous "Zionism is racism" resolution remains a landmark in the annals of passionate advocacy. As for the wit, well, asked once whether it was true that he had been sick throughout his years as ambassador to India, Pat replied, "I was only sick once. It lasted two and a half years!"

For all of these reasons, it seemed to some of us, in the late 1970s, that Pat was singularly positioned to do several things at once: save the Democratic Party from its nosedive into the fever swamps of the Sixties; bring a new bipartisan realism to social welfare policy; remind us that a healthy culture was important for democracy; and give America back a sense of itself as a protagonist of the history of freedom. In doing this, he might have uniquely embodied, in our high politics, the insights of Catholic social doctrine and the Catholic optic on world affairs.

Alas, it was not to be. For whatever reasons—New York state politics and fear of the then-influential *New York Times* likely high among them—Pat did virtually nothing about the great civil rights issue of the late twentieth century: the defense of the right to life. He once famously said that, while everyone is entitled to his own opinion, no one is entitled to his own facts. And no one as intelligent as Daniel Patrick Moynihan could have been ignorant of the scientific facts about the product of human conception, the moral facts about the ethical status of the preborn child, and the jurisprudential facts about the travesty of legal reasoning that produced *Roe v. Wade*, arguably the worst Supreme Court decision since *Dred Scott*. Yet, until an end-of-career vote against partial-birth abortion, Pat Moynihan was not a happy warrior for life, as he had been a happy warrior for other great causes.

This was more than a sadness, involving one man's failure of insight and nerve. It marked, I believe, the greatest lost opportunity to bring the full range of Catholic insights to bear in public life in my lifetime. All of America, and not just Catholics, suffers from that lost opportunity, still.

"Xavier Rynne"

Francis X. Murphy, C.Ss.R. (1915–2002)

No reporter or op-ed columnist ever refers to the Dalai Lama as a liberal Buddhist or a conservative Buddhist. I suspect that's because everyone understands that Buddhism is far too complex and subtle a religious tradition to be analyzed in simplistic political categories. What, then, accounts for the near-universal journalistic addiction to parsing every Catholic issue, and every Catholic personality, in these terms?

There are undoubtedly lots of explanations, but a considerable amount of the credit, or blame, for this taxonomic convention must go to Father Francis X. Murphy, a Redemptorist priest who wrote a series of reports for the *New Yorker* on the Second Vatican Council under the pseudonym "Xavier Rynne". Prior to the Council, virtually no one described the Church or churchmen as "liberal" or "conservative", despite the fact that there were well-defined (and often contentious) factions, reflecting different theological casts of mind, in pre–Vatican II Catholicism. After the Council, which is to say after Xavier Rynne's chatty *New Yorker* reports on the Council (which were later compiled in four books), everything in the Church was suddenly liberal or conservative.

This has caused endless mischief. Doctrine isn't liberal or conservative. Doctrine is true, or it's heresy. Theology isn't liberal or conservative, either. Theology is thoughtful or dumb, scholarly or shoddy, well-informed or ill-informed. To treat doctrine or theology as essentially political matters distorts the Church's self-understanding, divides the Church into silos, and promotes the pernicious view that every issue in the Church is, at bottom, a question of power.

Having beaten this drum for years to little discernible effect, I was struck on rereading the first of the Xavier Rynne books, *Letters from Vatican City*, by its rather measured tone. Unlike the later Rynne books, which neatly divided the Council assembly into good guys (liberals) and bad guys (conservatives) and happily chose up sides between them (the liberals being the open-minded forces of desirable change and the conservatives being devious and haughty reactionaries), the Rynne of *Letters from Vatican City* went out of his way to explain the seemingly inexplicable Catholic commitment to authority and tradition to *New Yorker* readers in a sympathetic way, and in terms that a largely unchurched readership could grasp. Rynne even defended, gently, Pope Pius XII's 1950 encyclical *Humani Generis*, which publicists like Father Richard McBrien flagellated for decades as an unmitigated horror and an indefensible assault on theology.

What happened to Rynne between 1962 and 1965? Indeed, what happened to Rynne, protagonist of change, between 1965 and 1985, when he was heard to complain, during John Paul II's Extraordinary Synod marking the Council's twentieth anniversary, "Why do we have to change things?"

We'll never know for sure what happened to Xavier Rynne/ Francis X. Murphy, CSsR. But it may be that this engaging man, who was one of the great clerical raconteurs, fell into a pattern of thinking that was the mirror image of the conservatives he lambasted: he came to think of the Church primarily in institutional terms.

That the Church has an institutional structure is both obvious and necessary, for the Church exists in time and space. But the clear intention of Vatican II was to get the Church thinking of itself in something beyond institutional categories. Faced with a great civilizational crisis that had already produced two world wars, three totalitarian systems, and mass slaughter on an unprecedented scale, the Council asked the Church to rediscover Christianity as a great evangelical movement: the Bride of Christ, sent into the world by Christ to propose to the world both the truth about itself and the truth of God's passionate love for the world he created, which are the same truth. That, the Council suggested, was the best thing Catholicism could do for the modern world.

Institution-think is a tough habit to break. The habit has by no means been conquered by some Catholic traditionalists. But Catholic "progressives" are often just as much proponents of the Church-as-institution model today. This is a great reversal. And it is very sad.

I enjoyed Father Murphy's company the few times we met, and at his death I prayed for the repose of his soul—even as I hoped that he would, in the divine mercy, find himself in circumstances where the Church is, manifestly, neither liberal nor conservative.

Number 84
Jim Mutscheller (1930–2015)

He scored forty times in an eight-year NFL career, but he's best remembered for the touchdown he didn't score, as the sun set over Yankee Stadium on December 28, 1958, and his footing gave way on the frozen turf at the one-yard line. His wife of fifty-nine years, Joan, said that Jim Mutscheller wanted to be remembered as a man "who had led a good life", for he was "quiet, humble, and so conservative that he'd eat crabs with a suit and tie on". And therein lies a tale—and a yardstick by which to measure professional sports then and now.

Born in Beaver Falls, Pennsylvania (as was Joe Namath, about as different a personality type as can be imagined), Mutscheller's father was known locally as the "best bricklayer in Beaver County". The son graduated from Notre Dame, having played offensive and defensive end on the 1949 national championship team in those rugged days of single-platoon football. He then spent a couple of years in the Marine Corps—including a stint in Korea that convinced Mutscheller that getting knocked around on the football field wasn't so bad a deal after all.

He was a tight end in the days when you could be six feet tall, weigh 190, and play that position, what with no 350-pound behemoths on the other side of the line. But he was also reasonably fleet afoot; he could block, he had those great hands, and there was that look in his eyes (which, as sportswriter Tom Callahan put it, "could bore a hole in a vault"). All of which helped bring him and the Baltimore Colts to the Bronx on a bleak December afternoon in 1958, for what's now known as the Greatest Game Ever Played. It wasn't, in fact, all that great a game, as Mutscheller's teammate Artie Donovan admitted (in an autobiography with the classic title *Fatso*). But the game had a lot of drama; it ended with the first sudden-death overtime win in the history of NFL championships; and Jim Mutscheller was in the pivot of the action.

With strong men ready to collapse from exhaustion after four and a half quarters of play in dank, freezing weather, the Colts, having driven to the Giants' six-yard line, were poised for the game-winning touchdown. The great one, John Unitas, brought the Colts out of the huddle, having called a running play for "The Horse", Alan Ameche (who looked more like a tenor in a Verdi opera than a Heisman Trophy–winning fullback). Unitas, however, noticed a chink in the Giants' pass defense and checked off at the line of scrimmage, calling for Mutscheller to run an out pattern to the near corner of the end zone.

It was intended to be a touchdown pass and would have been except that Unitas deliberately led Mutscheller a bit more to the outside than usual, guarding against an interception by the Giants' defense; Number 84 couldn't get traction on the icy surface after reaching for and making the catch, slipping out of bounds three feet short of the end zone. On the next play, Ameche drove in for the winning score, with Mutscheller throwing a key block that took out Giants' linebacker Cliff Livingston. Years after the game that changed the way America spends Sunday afternoons from September through January, Unitas would kid Mutscheller, saying, "Geez, Jim, I tried to make you the hero." To which Mutscheller replied, "If I'd scored that touchdown, Ameche wouldn't have been able to sell all those hamburgers." (Extra credit for anyone who can remember the name of the double-stack burger at "Ameche's".)

They're almost all gone, now, these Catholic sports heroes of my extreme youth: Ameche first, in 1988; Unitas in 2002; Artie Donovan in 2013; Mutscheller, whom I used to see at daily Mass, head bowed after receiving the Mystery; Gino Marchetti in 2019. I sometimes think of them during the parade of oversized young studs, oozing self-esteem and entitlement, who walk across the stage to get their bro-hug from Commissioner Roger Goodell on the National Football League's draft day. And I remember that, once upon a time, Catholic men from working class families could be sports idols—and role models as well.

The Portavoce

Joaquín Navarro-Valls (1936–2017)

No knowledgeable student of modern Catholic history will dispute the claim that Joaquín Navarro-Valls was the most successful director of the Holy See Press Office in the history of that institution. The reasons why tell us something about this remarkable man, and about the pope he served, Saint John Paul II.

Navarro brought to the *Sala Stampa della Santa Sede* a distinctive set of skills and credentials. He was an intellectually sophisticated Catholic layman, well-formed in the Church's teaching, intellectually engaged by its theological explication, and committed to it as a way of life that led to happiness and, ultimately, to beatitude. He was a skilled professional in two demanding fields, psychiatry and journalism, and enjoyed the respect of his peers in both medicine and the press. He was an attractive personality, warm and humorous; yet he was also strong enough to make a sometimes-rowdy Vatican press corps behave itself and to push back skillfully against a sometimes recalcitrant Roman Curia. He did not panic in crises, and he was at his best when his job was most difficult. He had the confidence of the man for whom he worked, John Paul II, and they shared a mutual affection grounded in a common Catholic faith and mission.

Perhaps most importantly, Joaquín Navarro-Valls took up his position in 1984 knowing that change was imperative—and that John Paul II would support him in making the necessary changes in Vatican communications. A very accomplished curialist and John Paul's first secretary of state, Cardinal Agostino Casaroli, once said of the press, "We don't really care what they write as long as we can do what we want to do." That may have been the case when Cardinal Ercole Consalvi represented the Holy See at the Congress of Vienna in 1815, where he and others re-drew the map of Europe after the Napoleonic Wars—and did so without any public scrutiny. But the days of such aristocratic hegemony were long gone, and Navarro understood that what "they" wrote (and broadcast, and livestreamed, and put on the Internet) had a great deal to do with perceptions of what the Church taught and what the Church did. Those perceptions, in turn, shaped the terrain on which the Catholic Church had to work for the salvation of souls and the healing of the world in the late twentieth and early twenty-first centuries. Good media relations could help the Church tell its story, make its evangelical proposal, and help bend history's curve in a more humane direction. Bad media relations impeded the proclamation of the Gospel and created obstacles to the Church's action in world affairs. Knowing that, Joaquín Navarro-Valls became both a successful director of the Holy See Press Office and an influential member of John Paul II's inner team of counselors.

That the first layman to hold the position of papal spokesman could have had such an impact also tells us something about Saint John Paul II.

Karol Wojtyła was an extraordinary man in many ways, but especially in his ability to think "outside" his personal experience and perceive things one might not have thought him likely to understand. He was a devoted priest and bishop who did not divide the Church into separate boxes labeled "clergy" and "laity". He was a dedicated celibate with a profound understanding of the dynamics of human love, especially as experienced by women. He never lived in a mature democracy, but he had a keen understanding of the cultural conditions that make it possible for democracies to flourish. He lived outside the modern economy and never wrote checks or used a credit card; yet he grasped the dynamics of postindustrial economic life and reshaped the Church's social doctrine in a more empirically sensitive key. And while he spent his pre-papal adult life contending with the rigidly controlled and censored media of communist-era Poland, he intuitively understood the importance of the press and the broader media environment for the Church.

When Wojtyła was elected Bishop of Rome in 1978, the Vatican press operation was, to put it charitably, primitive, and seemed more interested in keeping the media at bay than in getting the Church's story told well. This was in part a function of the attitude expressed by Casaroli, that the press really doesn't count in the world of affairs; it was also a function of incompetence and laziness. Papal spokesmen were ill-prepared for their job because they had no experience relevant to doing the job. The mechanisms of the *Sala Stampa*, reflecting the languid, Italianate character of the Roman Curia, seemed to operate in slow motion and its personnel had no idea of how to anticipate news and thus help frame a story in a positive way. Joaquín Navarro-Valls was able to change that and to make the *Sala Stampa* an effective partner in the papacy's mission, because he and John Paul II shared a different idea of the Church and the papacy, rooted in the teaching of the Second Vatican Council and Navarro's experience as a numerary of Opus Dei.

As Navarro once put it to me, he and John Paul understood the relationship between the papacy and the media in dialectical terms. Vatican II had made it clear that the pope had to speak to the world as well as the Church; it had also taught that the pope is not a king but a man who emerges from the Church and the priesthood—so the pope is fundamentally a teacher and sanctifier of the world, not a politician operating as other world leaders. And what the world had to see in the pope, first and foremost, was the power of the sacraments at work within him. In order to display this power, the pope had to be open to media scrutiny, even as his spokesman had to explain the religious, philosophical, or theological rationale for why the pope did or said this or that to a press corps accustomed to thinking of a pope as another form of prime minister or president dressed in a distinctive outfit.

In an open, honest, professional relationship, Navarro understood, the press would be able to do its job while the pope would have new ways of getting his message out to the world and the Church. That this method could have a considerable impact on world politics was demonstrated by the role the Church and the Holy See (and Joaquín Navarro-Valls) played before and during the 1994 U.N. International Conference on Population and Development at Cairo and the 1995 Fourth World Conference on Women in Beijing; in both cases, effective Vatican communications and Navarro's unofficial diplomacy thwarted the efforts of major world powers to enshrine grave wrongs like abortion as "rights" under international law.

As I look back over the notes from many conversations with Joaquín Navarro-Valls, I am struck by the breadth of territory we covered as he helped me prepare both volumes of my John Paul II biography, *Witness to Hope* and *The End and the Beginning*.

At the beginning of our collaboration, Navarro was one of my guides through the labyrinth of the Roman Curia. He had a penetrating insight into its deeply ingrained institutional habits. And he helped me to understand that, at least at that moment in history, its lethargy and the curial reluctance to cooperate with a biographer like me were less a matter of rascality or corruption than they were of what he termed the "human environment" of Vatican life. Like John Paul, Navarro-Valls was quite aware of how shattering it had been for the Italians who dominated the Curia to lose the papacy, and how difficult it was for them to adjust to a non-Italian pope—and a Spanish layman as papal spokesman (not to mention an American as papal biographer). So it was best, he often suggested, to try to make the balky curial machinery work for you, even if that required a certain amount of massaging egos and even if the pace was slower than one would have liked.

This sometimes required great patience and forbearance. I remember being stunned when Navarro told me that the cardinal secretary of state who had succeeded Casaroli, Angelo Sodano, had said offhandedly, in Navarro's presence, that "the *stranieri* [foreigners] don't really fit in well here." Others might have vocally challenged such a crude observation; Navarro simply let it pass, even as it must have taught him an important lesson. At the same time, lines had to be drawn when lethargy became obstruction or when aristocratic snobbery threatened to impede John Paul's determination to make his house the Church's house, where he could meet the Church's people and get information he was unlikely to get from official channels. One curial monsignor, later a nuncio, complained of John Paul's constant meeting with various individuals and groups, saying that "this used to be a place of respect and good taste; now it's Campo dei Fiori." Navarro brushed that away, too, saying that of course it was Campo dei Fiori—old Rome's great open-air market—for the Church had to be in the world in order to convert it, and the pope had to know what was going on in the world in order to bear witness to Christ in it. In this sense, Joaquín Navarro-Valls understood what John Paul II meant by the "New Evangelization" long before the Pope used that phrase.

Navarro was my teacher in other ways. He confirmed my sense that the "holy conspiracy" theory about John Paul and Ronald Reagan, promoted by Carl Bernstein and Marco Politi, was "rubbish" (a favorite Navarro word for nonsense): John Paul and President Reagan had pursued "parallel paths" toward a peaceful resolution of the Cold War, but their methods were quite different. Navarro explained to me how, with respect to the papacy and Italian politics, John Paul II had "broadened the Tiber", extracting the Curia and the Italian bishops from their machinations in local and national politics and challenging the Italian Church to reconvert Italy—a task in which the Polish pope took a leading role.

He was perhaps most helpful in deepening my understanding of how John Paul conducted his life and his papacy. The Pope's intense prayer life and insatiable intellectual curiosity led him to spend a long time trying to understand a problem or issue from the inside, before attempting to address it. John Paul was a master of time management who lived his days in carefully scheduled minutes. He understood the importance of the medicine of humor when things got difficult, and he was determined not to let the old-fashioned bureaucratic machinery he had inherited depress him—or change his conviction about his obligations. John Paul's ability to focus on the things he really cared about, rather than letting himself be ground down by internal opposition or curial incompetence, was another aspect of his pontificate that Navarro underscored: focusing on the big picture, rather than bureaucratic trivia, kept the pontificate moving forward when it might otherwise have stalled or ground to a halt.

Perhaps my most fascinating conversations with Joaquín Navarro-Valls involved his role as an unofficial papal diplomat, working in Cuba to make arrangements for John Paul II's historic visit to that island-prison in January 1998.

Fidel Castro was not an easy man to deal with, but Navarro seems to have handled him with grace, wit, and just enough toughness to gain the Cuban dictator's respect. Told to address Castro as "Commandante", Navarro insisted on calling him "Mr. President"—a clear signal to the Cubans that, as he put it later to me, "I'm not going to play on your linguistic or ideological turf." When the discussion turned to the January 1998 visit, Navarro deftly put the burden of the visit's outcome on the man known as *El Jefe*, saying that the papal visit was a fact and that "it is in the interest of Cuba that this visit be a great success—Cuba should surprise the world." That appeal to Castro's vanity seemed to work. When Navarro followed up by raising the question of Christmas 1997 being a public holiday for the first time since the Cuban Revolution, Castro balked, saying that it was sugarcane-harvesting season and he couldn't let people off work. Once again, Navarro knew which card to play: "But the Pope would like to thank you publicly for this when he arrives at the Havana airport." *El Jefe* conceded, muttering that "it's just for this year," and Navarro, who knew when to accept victory quietly, quickly replied, "Fine, we are grateful; we shall let next year take care of itself." When Castro said that getting visas for priests wanting to come to Cuba before the visit would take time, Navarro said that they were needed immediately to help prepare the people and make the papal visit a success. Castro asked, "How many do you need?" Navarro, who admitted to me that he was taking a stab in the dark, replied, "Half of those on the waiting list." And a few days later, fifty-seven visas were granted: exactly half of those on the waiting list.

These exchanges on issues, which lasted long into the small hours of the morning, were punctuated by the standard Castro jeremiads about American aggression, the American trade embargo, the evils of capitalism, the glories of the Cuban Revolution, and so forth. Navarro, who as a Spaniard and a psychiatrist had a keen sense of important aspects of Castro's character, thought that the Cuban's "exaggerated sense of honor" made him a "prisoner of his own history" for whom it was too late, personally and historically, to stop fighting what he had been fighting for decades, no matter how unsuccessfully. This did not make Castro any less responsible for his crimes; but it did suggest that the way to make January 1998 a success for the Church and John Paul II, and to open up some space for freedom in Cuba, was to work with, rather than against, the grain of Castro's pride and passions. Thus Navarro turned to advantage the information he had gotten from various ambassadors to Havana, that their governments were waiting until the end of January (1998) to redefine their policy toward Cuba. Casually mentioning this to Castro, as if it were something the dictator obviously knew already, Navarro thus gained more leverage for Cuban cooperation, with the regime allowing people to come to papal events freely and broadcasting the events on Cuban radio and television.

In Cuba, the layman and informal intermediary, Navarro, was able to accomplish more than conventional papal diplomacy could likely have achieved. But he was not above letting the Cuban dictator know that sycophancy was not a tactic he would ever adopt. So at three o'clock one morning, after six hours of negotiation, a bleary-eyed papal spokesman said to the Cuban dictator, as Castro was seeing him out, "Mr. President, your great mistake was not making Coca-Cola the official sponsor of the Cuban Revolution." *El Jefe*, to whom no one had spoken that way in forty years, laughed.

In the final analysis, Joaquín Navarro-Valls was an extraordinarily successful papal spokesman and unofficial diplomat because he and the pope he served shared a common vision of the Church's role in the late modern world and of how Catholicism's evangelical mission (which included the Church's public witness with both dictators and democrats) could be advanced by a carefully crafted and skillfully executed communications strategy. They also trusted each other, spoke regularly, and could explore issues, personalities, and strategies together within a bond of friendship and confidence. Any future pope and future director of the Holy See Press Office looking for a template to make Vatican communications work in service to the Church's mission need look no farther than the historic—and historically consequential—partnership between Pope Saint John Paul II and Dr. Joaquín Navarro-Valls.

First Things First
Richard John Neuhaus (1936–2009)

The conventional story line on Father Richard John Neuhaus is that his eventful life was defined by change, transition, even rupture: Lutheran pastor's kid becomes teenage hellion becomes Lutheran pastor becomes Catholic priest; Democratic congressional candidate becomes adviser to Republican presidents; Sixties radical becomes Eighties neoconservative. And truth to tell (as he would say), there was at least something to this.

The early influences on his adult religious thought and sensibility included the Lutheran theologian Arthur Carl Piepkorn (who taught him to think of Lutheranism as a reform movement within the one Church of Christ) and Rabbi Abraham Joshua Heschel (from whom he drew the idea that Christianity and Judaism were necessarily locked into a conversation from which both ought to benefit); his later interlocutors in matters theological included the German Lutheran Wolfhart Pannenberg (whom he helped introduce to the English-speaking world), Joseph Ratzinger (later Pope Benedict XVI), and Pope John Paul II.

He worked with Martin Luther King, Jr., and Ralph David Abernathy in the classic period of the American civil rights movement; his chastisement of William F. Buckley, Jr., in a letter complaining about *National Review*'s stance on civil rights legislation, led to lunch and then to thirty years of friendship, conversation, and collaboration.

He was typically labeled a "conservative" Catholic in his latter years; yet for more than four decades, he was at the intellectual center of both the ecumenical and interreligious dialogues, in partnership with a diverse crew that included, at various moments, Cardinal Avery Dulles, S.J.; William Sloane Coffin, Jr.; Charles W. Colson; Father Alexander Schmemann; Stanley Hauerwas; Gilbert Meilaender; Timothy George; Rabbi David Novak; and Rabbi Leon Klenicki.

He was an early supporter of Jimmy Carter, who became a counselor to George W. Bush; with the sociologist Peter Berger, he proposed a new way of thinking about "mediating structures" (or voluntary associations) in society, thereby providing the intellectual foundation for Bush's faith-based and community initiatives.

He was a vocal critic of America's war in Southeast Asia, who helped cause a major rift in the postwar peace movement by criticizing the persecution of religious believers by the communist government of a unified Vietnam.

His friends and familiars included prominent American public intellectuals of all faiths and no faith; on two different days, he could be found arguing amiably and intensely with Henry Kissinger about morality and foreign policy, and then with Norman Podhoretz about the proper interpretation of Isaiah and Saint Paul.

In tandem with colleagues like Michael Novak and Robert Benne, he made a Christian moral case for the superiority of the free market over socialism; yet by his own choice, most of his pastoral work as both Lutheran pastor and Catholic priest was in poor and working-class parishes.

He loved music, especially Bach, and he loved to sing; but he couldn't carry a tune to save his life.

He was a brilliant preacher and a wonderful raconteur who also suffered through his dark nights.

Anyone whose journey through this world spanned that range of experiences and touched that wide a cast of characters obviously went through some changes over time. As I reflect on thirty-one years of friendship and common work with Richard Neuhaus, however, I'm far more impressed by the consistencies than by the discontinuities in his life and thought.

To begin with, he was a thoroughgoing Christian radical, meaning that he believed that the truth of Christian faith was not just truth-for-Christians, but the truth of the world, period. As with his hero John Paul II (and contrary to the conventional wisdom on "tolerance"), that basic, unshakeable conviction opened him up to serious conversation with others, rather than shutting down the argument. Yet his fundamental theological convictions, and the intellectual sophistication he brought to their defense, had resonances far beyond the boundaries of the religious world, for those convictions also undergirded the two big ideas that he put into play in American public life.

The first of these ideas, laid out in his 1984 bestseller, *The Naked Public Square*, involved that hardy perennial in the garden of American controversy, Church and state. Neuhaus' position was that the two pieces of the First Amendment's provisions on religious freedom were in fact one "religion clause", in which "no establishment" of religion served the "free exercise" of religion. There was to be no established national church, precisely in order to create the free space for the robust exchange of religious ideas and the free expression of religious practices. In making this case, Neuhaus changed the terms of the contemporary American Church-state debate, arguing that the Supreme Court had been getting things wrong for more than half a century by pitting "no establishment" against "free exercise", with the latter increasingly being forced into the constitutional back seat. It was a bold proposal from a theologian that has been increasingly vindicated by legal and historical scholarship on Supreme Court Church-state jurisprudence, and by several SCOTUS decisions in the years after his death.

Neuhaus' convictions about the meaning of religious freedom in America also reflected his consistent defense of popular piety and the religious sensibilities of those whom others might consider "simple" or "uninformed". If 90 percent of the American people professed belief in the God of the Bible, he argued, then there was something profoundly undemocratic about denying those people—a supermajority if ever there was one—the right to bring the sources of their deepest moral convictions into public debate, even if they sometimes did so in clumsy ways.

That populism was also at the root of Neuhaus' second big idea: that the pro-life movement was in moral continuity with the classic civil rights movement, because pro-life claims were rooted in the same moral truths for which he had marched with King and Abernathy across the Edmund Pettis Bridge outside Selma, Alabama. The pro-life position, Neuhaus insisted, was a matter of the first principles of justice, and those principles could not be sacrificed to what some imagined to be the imperatives of the sexual revolution. Thus as early as 1967, he warned his liberal and radical friends that their advocacy of "abortion rights" was a betrayal of their previous commitments.

For to deny the unborn the right to life was to shrink the community of common protection and concern in America, whereas the whole point of the civil rights insurgency had been to enlarge that community by finally including African Americans within it.

On a related set of questions, Neuhaus was also concerned with elitism and its corrosive effects on the poor people he served. He often spoke of his experience of reading an early essay on "quality of life", back in the embryonic days of what would eventually come to be known as bioethics. The author described "quality of life" in terms of income, education, recreational opportunities, and so forth; then, as Neuhaus told the story, "I got into my pulpit on Sunday, looked out at the congregation, and realized that not a single person there had what was being described as 'quality of life'." Something was seriously wrong; and so the dignity of every human life, not its alleged "quality", became the conceptual basis on which he entered the bioethics struggles that now define such a significant part of the national agenda.

Both of these Big Ideas—no war between "free exercise" and "no establishment", and the pro-life movement as the natural moral successor to the civil rights movement—intersected in what Richard Neuhaus, public intellectual, thought of as his life's project: the creation of a "religiously informed public philosophy for the American experiment in ordered liberty", as he frequently put it. Understanding each of the pieces of that puzzle is important to understanding the man.

A "religiously informed public philosophy" was one that took account of the American people's abiding religiosity, but "translated" biblically informed moral convictions into a language that people of different faiths or no faith could engage. The American "experiment", for Neuhaus, was an unfinished, and indeed never to be finished, political project. American public life, as he understood it, was a constant testing of whether a nation "so conceived and so dedicated" could "long endure"; thus Lincoln's question at Gettysburg was a question for every generation of Americans, not just the generation of the Civil War. And then there was "ordered liberty", in which the adjective captured Neuhaus' conviction (which paralleled that of the classic English liberal and historian of freedom, Lord Acton) that political liberty was not a matter of doing whatever we like, but of having the right to do what we ought.

Richard John Neuhaus' lifelong habit of serious conversation—typically complemented by bourbon and cigars—was fed by his voracious reading. The breadth of his professional reading was on display every month in his personal section of *First Things*, the magazine he launched in the early 1990s; fittingly enough, the section was styled "Public Square", and its large readership marveled at the amount of material that Neuhaus read, digested, and commented on every four weeks. Our twenty-two years of vacationing together at his cottage on the Ottawa River introduced me to the more personal side of my friend's unquenchable thirst for challenging ideas, preferably couched in good writing: one year, he would read Macauley's history of England; another year, it would be Gibbon's *Decline and Fall of the Roman Empire*; yet another, Aquinas' *Summa Theologiae*. And on at least three occasions during those two decades, he read through virtually all of Shakespeare.

Yet the same man could spend the late evenings howling with laughter over DVDs of *Talladega Nights*, *Best in Show*, or *A Mighty Wind*. (Lest I create scandal, I should add that he also appreciated serious movies, and that his leisure reading included mystery writers such as P. D. James and Ellis Peters. If memory serves, he also claimed to have read *Scoop*, Evelyn Waugh's send-up of journalism, at least ten times.)

The public world, where he spent much of his working life as writer and editor, thought of him as a controversialist, which he surely was (and a very skillful one at that). But what the public world rarely saw was the man who spent countless hours counseling young people, or receiving unannounced and uninvited visitors to his office who just "had to meet Father Neuhaus", or hearing confessions and celebrating Mass in his parish. He could be fierce, rhetorically; but those whom he led through the thickets of religious quandaries, vocational discernments, or psychological crises knew him to be remarkably patient and gentle. And so, while he was arguably the most consequential American religious intellectual since Reinhold Niebuhr and John Courtney Murray, his memory will long be cherished by people who knew little or nothing of his public life but did know him to be a man of conviction, conscience, and compassion—a true pastor.

Which is no bad way for the man who dubbed his poor Bedford-Stuyvesant parish "St. John the Mundane" to be remembered.

A Tzaddik *for the* World
Michael Novak (1933–2017)

Michael Novak loved the Catholic Church and the United States passionately. And with his death, both Church and nation lost one of their most imaginative and accomplished sons: a groundbreaking theorist in philosophy, social ethics, religious studies, ethnic studies, and economics; a brilliant teacher; a winsome journalist and apologist; a great defender of freedom, as both ambassador and polemicist; a man of striking energy and creativity, some of whose books will be read for a very long time to come, and in multiple languages.

In his last weeks, however, my thoughts turned, not to Michael's scholarly and literary accomplishments, which others will rightly celebrate, but to various adventures we shared. Some of them may shed light on aspects of his character that might have escaped the attention of his admirers, as they certainly escaped the attention of his detractors.

Shortly after his best-known book, *The Spirit of Democratic Capitalism*, was published, I arranged for Michael to address a dinner meeting of the twenty top executives of Seattle-First National Bank. Seattle, in those days, had not yet become a contestant for Most Politically Correct City on Planet Earth, and I doubt that many of the Seafirst leadership imagined themselves to be anything other than bottom-line businessmen, skeptical of intrusions by intellectuals into their domain. Yet within a half-hour, Mike had them thinking of themselves, and enterprise, in an entirely new way: as a moral system, a human ecology, in which habits of the mind and heart counted for as much as balance sheets. Terms like "sin", "pluralism", "practical wisdom", and "the communitarian individual" were not staples, I dare say, in Seafirst executive dining-room conversations before that night. But over the course of three hours I saw Michael Novak make men of financial and economic power think—and think of themselves as called to a noble vocation, subject like all other vocations to temptations and very much in need of redemption.

When I moved to Washington, D.C., the following year, I quickly came to see how Michael Novak and his good friend James Billington, then the director of the Woodrow Wilson International Center for Scholars, were making the nation's capital an environment in which religiously informed moral reason was in play as in no other great world center. Jim Billington did this by quietly ensuring that the Wilson Center's fellows included theologians and religious philosophers with a feel for applying their craft to the contingencies of political life, and then putting them in touch with the town's movers and shakers. Michael did it by being himself in conversation with a wide range of Washingtonians, and by helping make the American Enterprise Institute a think tank where the software side of the democratic project was scrutinized for its weaknesses—and where possible improvements, informed by the biblical view of the human person, were imagined. There was nothing like that, then, in London or Paris; and there isn't today. But there is in Washington, and that is in no small part due to the work and the personal example of Michael Novak.

Then there was a memorably dreadful evening in Naples: Italy, not Florida.

In the early 1990s, Michael, Richard John Neuhaus, and I all had books published in Italian editions by Mondadori, and the firm's chief, the estimable Leonardo Mondadori (whose ardent Catholicism coincided with a social circle that included Bianca Jagger), insisted that we all come to Italy for presentations of our books in various forums.

The Roman event presenting our translated books, geared to the Italian press, took place in the Collegio Teutonico inside the Vatican and was my first introduction to the fact that the border between fact and fiction in Italian journalism is, to put it gently, porous. Richard was talking about his book on John Paul II's great social encyclical, *Centesimus Annus*; Michael was talking about his new book on Catholic social thought; I was talking about my book on John Paul II's role in the collapse of European communism, *The Final Revolution*; yet in Italy's newspaper of record, the *Corriere della Sera*, all of this was presented as a devious plot to gin up support for playboy-gazillionaire-turned-politician Silvio Berlusconi.

Even worse awaited us in Naples, where Leonardo Mondadori had arranged for a more academically focused session at which three Italian professors would discuss our books with us, and then with the audience. Or so we thought. The event was held in a restored monastery in the hills above the city, but despite the altitude the room was infernally hot and the Italian colleagues were infernally long-winded. An hour and a half into the program, neither Michael, nor Richard, nor I had said a word, and Richard's patience was wearing thin. When the Italian academics finally quieted down, Richard began by saying that, given the hour and the temperature, he would follow the dominical injunction to "be merciful as your heavenly Father is merciful" (see Lk 6:36) and confine his remarks to five minutes; I followed suit. But Michael, sensing that something more was expected of us, saved the evening by talking with great clarity and precision about the contributions John Paul II had made to Catholic social doctrine, explaining how these contributions ought to be of interest to even the most anti-clerical Italians. It was a bravura performance, and a lesson in patience and perseverance that I tried to follow in the years ahead.

And there was Michael Novak, sports fan.

It must have been in the mid-1980s when I took Michael to old Memorial Stadium in Baltimore for an Orioles game on a glorious late-spring evening. There was one feature of that old brick-and-concrete horseshoe that never failed to move me: as you came up one of the cement ramps to the upper deck, you caught a glimpse of the infield and a part of the outfield beneath the overhanging mezzanine section of the ballpark. That first sight of the greensward each season was always redolent of renewal, and Michael and I shared a sense of vernal reawakening, complemented by the sharp crack of a batting-practice ball leaving an ash bat and heading for the bleachers. "Greatest sound in sports," I said. "Except for 'swish'," Michael immediately replied, thus revealing himself as a hoops man at heart.

I've watched countless hours of games with a vast number of people over the past six decades, on site or on television—but I have never met anyone, anywhere, who got such intense pleasure out of sports as Michael Novak. And not "intense" in the Bill Belichick sense of the clenched-jaw scowl, but "intense" as in sheer pleasure. Michael being Michael, that passion for our games overflowed into his writing, including the book he wanted to call *Balls* until an antsy editor talked him into something a little more, er, delicate: *The Joy of Sports*. But whatever the title, it was a book replete with insights that could only come from a passionate fan who had played the games and then thought seriously about them: baseball's freedom from clock time as a signal of transcendence and its unique combination of individual achievement and team play as the embodiment of the "communitarian individual", football as "the liturgy of the bureaucratic state". The thought of never having the opportunity to watch another game with him, swapping stories and second-guessing managers and coaches, is not a happy one. But if heaven is the perfection of earthly goods, we'll pick up the conversation in a place without instant replay, because the umps and refs always get it right.

And finally there was Michael Novak, teacher.

In 1992, Michael started a summer seminar in Catholic social thought, which he handed over to me in 1999 and that continues, decades later, in Kraków. As various ailments began to wear away at his physical capacities, Michael stopped coming, Kraków not being a city very friendly to people with difficulties getting about. But a few years before his death he asked if he could participate again, if just for a few days, and I readily agreed. The economics section of the program, of which he was once the star, was being covered by others, so Michael spoke about his first love, philosophy, and the modern experience of nothingness. He was not a histrionic lecturer, but his soft and rather high voice, surprising when you first heard it coming from such a big man, had a mesmerizing quality, and my colleagues on the faculty began to understand why Michael was voted teacher of the year two of the three years he taught at Stanford.

But it was less his lectures than his interactions with our students— young North Americans and Central Europeans, all doing graduate studies—that I found most striking. They vied to push his wheelchair along the cobblestoned sidewalks of the city and jammed small restaurants to have lunch with him. He always had time for any number of questions. And in addition to what he brought to our work intellectually, he offered a model of patient counseling and courteous listening that our students will long remember.

It was only then, more than thirty years after we had first begun to collaborate, that I came to understand that Michael—author, intellectual, diplomat, counselor to presidents, and friend of a pope—was first and foremost a teacher. What gave him the greatest satisfaction was seeing others get the light of understanding in their eyes and the joy of discovery on their faces. He would, I think, be willing to be judged by the world on that, his vocation as a teacher—and the judgment, if just, would be a very favorable one.

At the end of Chaim Potok's novel *The Chosen*, the Hasidic sage, Reb Saunders, concedes to his son Danny's determination to become a psychologist and says that the gifted young man he had hoped would succeed him in the rabbinate would be a *"tzaddik* for the world"—a healing teacher. That was Michael Novak's vocation, too. Those who never grasped that missed a great deal of what was best about American Catholicism in the late twentieth and early twenty-first centuries. Those of us who benefited immensely from his friendship and tutelage remember him with affection and gratitude.

The Polish American Knight
Jan Nowak-Jeziorański (1915–2005)

The ideal knight—courageous and honest, courteous and modest, loyal and pure of heart—isn't easy to find in any time or place. Yet I once knew such a man: Jan Nowak-Jeziorański, who died at age ninety-one on January 20, 2005, in Warsaw, a city reborn from beneath the rubble of modernity's two worst tyrannies.

Jan's story was beyond a scriptwriter's imagination. Born in Poland in 1913 and christened Zdisław Jeziorański, he studied business and economics and anticipated a professional career until Germany invaded his country in September 1939 and laid it under draconian occupation. Jeziorański joined the Polish underground Home Army as a courier, morphed into "Jan Nowak" (the Polish equivalent of "John Smith"), and put his linguistic skills, cool wits, and unshakeable courage at the service of his hard-pressed nation, crisscrossing Europe in disguise to bring news of Poland's resistance to the Polish government-in-exile in London and to Poland's British allies.

It was Jan who told the West about the 1943 Warsaw Ghetto Uprising, and Jan who came to London to brief Churchill on plans for the Polish Home Army's August 1944 Warsaw Uprising; after a depressing interview with the great British prime minister, Jan knew that little help would be coming for the brave Poles, from either the Royal Air Force or the Polish parachute brigade then in England (and about to be sacrificed at Arnhem). Undaunted, he returned to Warsaw to take part in the uprising, barely escaping death on numerous occasions. When it became completely hopeless, Jan and his wife, Jadwiga Wolska (a wartime bride he had married in a clandestine ceremony), escaped through the dying city's foul sewers and got out to the West, where Jan began a new life working for the British Broadcasting Corporation.

In 1956, Jan Nowak took over Radio Free Europe's Polish section, where his talents contributed to combating the lies of the other great twentieth-century totalitarian power, the Soviet Union. For twenty years, Jan Nowak was the "voice" of Radio Free Europe (RFE) in Poland; Pope John Paul II told Jan, on meeting him, that he'd long listened (illegally) to Jan's news broadcasts while shaving in the morning. Indeed, Poles of a certain age will tell you that, for two decades, Jan Nowak was the man who told them the truth about Poland and about the world, for RFE told the Poles what the government-controlled media wouldn't tell them.

I met Jan in the 1980s in Washington, where he served for almost twenty years as executive director of the Polish American Congress. During that time, he worked hard to improve Polish-Jewish relations and during the Carter administration served as a consultant to the National Security Council, led by Zbigniew Brzezinski. During the Reagan years, Jan was an informal and valued counselor to the president, the State Department, and AFL-CIO leader Lane Kirkland, who played a crucial role in supporting the Solidarity movement. President Clinton awarded Jan Nowak the Presidential Medal of Freedom, America's highest civilian honor, in 1996.

Jan was a remarkable combination of conviction and modesty. His judgments on men and affairs were clear-eyed and judicious; he could be critical, but without drawing blood. Utterly trustworthy himself, he reposed trust in those with whom he talked, on and off the record, about his role in some of the most dramatic events of our time. His countryman, the Polish pope, esteemed him. Recuperating in 1981 from Agca's assassination attempt and told by his doctors to read something that wasn't business, John Paul II chose Jan's memoir, *Courier from Warsaw*. There are few other contemporary volumes I would rather give a young man to teach him what manliness truly is.

My last conversation with Jan took place in July 2004; I was teaching in Kraków and called him at the Warsaw apartment to which he had moved in 2002, after "Greta", his wife of fifty-five years, whom all Washington knew by her Home Army code name, died. He seemed tired but was courteous as always, eager for whatever news I had. Just a few weeks before, he had enthralled dozens of Polish Dominican novices with stories of his adventures; those stories always illustrated, one way or another, his profound Catholic faith. When he died, the entire Polish parliament stood for a spontaneous minute of silent tribute to a knight-hero whom the entire country respected.

In Jan Nowak, Poland and America "met" as they hadn't since the days of Kościuszko and Pułaski. His life was a blessing to two peoples. Both honor themselves by revering his memory.

The Hillbilly Thomist as Apologist
Flannery O'Connor (1925–1964)

August 3, 2014, marked the golden anniversary of Flannery O'Connor's "Passover", to adopt the biblical image John Paul II used to describe the Christian journey through death to eternal life. In the years since lupus erythematosus claimed her at age thirty-nine, O'Connor's literary accomplishment has been widely celebrated. With the 1979 publication of *The Habit of Being*, her collected letters, another facet of O'Connor's genius came into focus: Mary Flannery O'Connor was an exceptionally gifted apologist, an explicator of Catholic faith who combined remarkable insight into the mysteries of the Creed with deep and unsentimental piety, unblinking realism about the Church in its human aspect, puckish humor—and a mordant appreciation of the soul-withering acids of modern secularism.

Insofar as I'm aware, there's never been an effort to initiate a beatification cause for Flannery O'Connor. If such a cause should ever be introduced, *The Habit of Being*, the letters collected in the 2019 volume, *Good Things Out of Nazareth*, and the lectures found in the Library of America edition of her *Collected Works* should be the principal documentary evidence for considering her an exemplar of heroic virtue, worthy to be commended to the whole Church.

O'Connor's sense that ours is an age of nihilism—an age suffering from a crabbed sourness about the mystery of being itself—makes her an especially apt apologist for the post–Vatican II Church, not least because she also understood the evangelical sterility of the smiley-face, cheap-grace, balloons-and-banners Catholicism that would become rampant shortly after her death. In a 1955 letter to her friend Betty Hester, Flannery O'Connor looked straight into the dark mystery of Good Friday and in four sentences explained why the late modern world often finds it hard to believe:

The truth does not change according to our ability to stomach it emotionally. A higher paradox confounds emotion as well as reason and there are long periods in the lives of all of us, and of the saints, when the truth as revealed by faith is hideous, emotionally disturbing, downright repulsive. Witness the dark night of the soul in individual saints. Right now the whole world seems to be going through a dark night of the soul.

That darkness is rendered darker still by late modernity's refusal to recognize its own deepest need. For as O'Connor put it in a 1957 lecture, "Redemption is meaningless unless there is cause for it in the actual life we live, and for the last few centuries there has been operating in our culture the secular belief that there is no such cause."

A world indifferent to its need for redemption is not merely indifferent to the possibility of redemption; as secular Christophobia through the ages has demonstrated time and again, it's a world hostile to that possibility. The mockery endured by Christ on the Cross may stand as the paradigmatic expression of that hostility.

The Church meets this hostility by doubling down on its conviction that the truths it professes are really true, and in fact reveal the deepest truth of the human condition. Flannery O'Connor again:

The virgin birth, the incarnation, the resurrection ... are the true laws of the flesh and the physical. Death, decay, destruction are the suspension of those laws. ... [It] would never have occurred to human consciousness to conceive of purity if we were not to look forward to a resurrection of the body, which will be flesh and spirit united in peace, in the way they were in Christ. The resurrection of Christ seems the high point in the law of nature.

You can't get much more countercultural than that. Yet what Miss O'Connor wrote speculatively in 1955 was what the Fathers of the Second Vatican Council solemnly affirmed a decade later, in *Gaudium et Spes*, the Pastoral Constitution on the Church in the Modern World: "In the mystery of the Word made flesh ... the mystery of man truly becomes clear. ... Christ the Lord, Christ the new Adam ... fully reveals man to himself and brings to light his most high calling."

Our postmodern age habitually thinks low. Flannery O'Connor, the self-styled "Hillbilly Thomist" whose fiction explored the darker crevices of the human condition, nevertheless invited us to think high—very high. She did so because she knew that the Resurrection changed both history and the cosmos. And as Christ is risen, so shall his faithful people be.

The Conscientious Washington Lawyer
Robert C. Odle, Jr. (1944–2019)

Thanksgiving along the Potomac littoral seemed a little emptier in 2019 without Rob Odle, who died eight weeks before the national holiday after a tough fight with cancer. But I'm sure that everyone who knew and esteemed him remembered to give thanks for his life among us swamp creatures. For Rob was the kind of person who humanized an often-tough town by his decency, his generosity, and the gentlemanly way he spoke his convictions without compromise, but also without rancor.

Despite two periods of service as a subcabinet officer at the U.S. Department of Housing and Urban Development and the U.S. Department of Energy, Rob Odle was not a man for the public limelight—a circumstance he not only cultivated but doubtless enjoyed. For his first experience of the glare of publicity came when, as director of administration for the Committee to Re-elect the President, he was the first on-camera witness at the Sam Ervin–led Watergate hearings. Rob was as squeaky clean as squeaky clean comes—one of his best friends told me that he was known in that expletive-deleted White House as "Richard Nixon's choirboy"—so there was never any question of his being involved in the skullduggery that eventually led to President Nixon's resignation. But for all that he might strike the ignorant as a Midwest innocent who somehow found himself in the Big Time, he was anything but that. He knew how the game was played in Washington, which meant that he knew that politics is a contact sport—decades after the Watergate mess, he told me that, when he first heard about the break-in, he immediately sensed that big trouble was just around the corner and braced himself for it at the bar of "1789", a Georgetown restaurant, "with six martinis".

It may have been the only night in his life that Rob Odle was, as they say, "overly served", for everything about the man bespoke moderation—except for his great love for Lydia, to whom he was married for fifty years, and his devotion to his son, John Paul, whom he brought to Rome in April 2005 so the boy could experience the funeral Mass of the saint for whom he'd been named after Rob and Lydia adopted him from Russia. And as I look back on twenty-plus years of friendship with him, it occurs to me that there was one other immoderation in Rob Odle's life: his passionate commitment to the Catholic Church, to which he had converted.

Rob brought the best of the Anglicanism in which he had been raised to his Catholicism, including an aesthetic sense that led him to generously support impressive works of art in parish churches. And while he shared many of his friends' concerns about the travails of the Church in the second decade of the twenty-first century, he never wavered in his commitment, for he knew that the Catholic Church had been through rough patches before. So, he got on with his volunteer service as an extraordinary minister of Holy Communion, bringing the consolation of the Eucharist to the sick and to shut-ins, and his work on the Review Board of the Diocese of Arlington, Virginia, to which he brought the insight and skills of a thoroughly professional attorney in assessing allegations of clerical sexual abuse.

Rob Odle was a conservative in the best sense of the term: he was devoted to what Russell Kirk called the "permanent things" and tried his best to make law, public policy, and government serve those permanent things. But unlike those frantic souls who seem to have forgotten that the permanent things are, well, permanent, Rob was never as anxious about the conservative future as others. So, he could work hard at helping rebuild the shattered economics of the post–Soviet Baltic states, confident as he was that there were economic truths built into the world, just like moral truths, and if you let those economic truths work, individuals and societies would flourish. Our conversations over two decades touched a wide variety of issues and personalities, but rarely Rob's own work—with the sole exception of what he was doing with the Baltic-American Enterprise Fund, helping entrepreneurs rebuild Lithuania, Latvia, and Estonia, which he described with enthusiasm and satisfaction.

The nation's capital is replete with lawyers and thus lawyer-jokes (most of them uncomplimentary). Rob Odle was a sterling exception to the world of legal gamesmanship (and, on occasion, sleaze). And it was, and is, attorneys like him who make Washington work, when it does. He served his clients well, generously made his firm's pro bono capacities available to a host of nonprofit organizations, conducted his own philanthropy with generosity and modesty, and brought uncommon good sense to any discussions of public policy in which he found himself. There are more Washington-based attorneys like that than the stereotypes and jokes would allow, and they are essential to both national governance and local comity. Their number was sadly diminished by Rob Odle's death. But the example of this conscientious and decent man (whose personal model was Saint Thomas More) will continue to inspire those in the capital for whom "public service" is just that: service, and not a ticket-punch to the higher altitudes of billable hours.

Arne Panula (1946–2017)

Easter reminds us that the Church begins with witness: lives changed by an encounter with the Risen Lord; men and women who then transform others by the power of their testimony and the authority of their example.

The Gospels are remarkably candid about the difficulty the first Christian witnesses had in grasping just what they had experienced. In John's gospel, Mary Magdalene confuses the Risen One with a gardener (20:14–15). In Luke's Resurrection account, two disciples walk a considerable distance on the Emmaus Road without recognizing their risen and glorified companion (24:13–35). In the Johannine epilogue, seven apostles on the Sea of Tiberias take a while to grasp that it's the Risen Lord who's cooking breakfast on the seashore (21:1–14).

This candor about initial incomprehension bears its own witness to the historicity of the Resurrection. For what happened on the first Easter Sunday was so completely unprecedented and yet so completely real that it exploded the expectations of pious Jews about history, the Messiah, and the fulfillment of God's promises, even as it transformed hitherto timid followers of the Rabbi Jesus of Nazareth into zealous evangelists who set off from the edges of the Roman Empire to convert, over the next 250 years, a lot of the Mediterranean world.

The witness of radically converted lives has been the lifeblood of Christianity ever since, for at the bottom of the bottom line of Christian faith is the encounter with a person, the Risen Lord, Jesus Christ. Christianity is also about creed, doctrine, morals, worship, and all the rest—but it is fundamentally about friendship with Jesus Christ and the transformation that engenders. And when it ceases to be that, it becomes the lifeless husk we see in twenty-first-century Germany and other parts of dechristianized Western Europe. Where

Christianity lives today, against all cultural odds, it's because of witnesses like those initially confused souls in Judea and Galilee whose conversion began with life-shattering and life-changing encounters with the Risen One.

Which, shortly before Easter 2017, brought me to visit the man I always called "my favorite Finno-American priest": Father Arne Panula.

A 1967 graduate of Harvard College, young Arne Panula took a doctorate in theology at the University of Navarre in Pamplona, Spain, and was ordained a priest of the Prelature of the Holy Cross and Opus Dei. After a distinguished career as an elementary school, high school, and college chaplain, and service to his religious community, Father Arne Panula was named the director of the Catholic Information Center (CIC) in Washington, D.C., in 2007—an oasis of the spirit located right in the belly of the beast (or, if you prefer, smack-dab in the depths of the swamp): on K Street between 15th and 16th Streets, surrounded by lobbyists, lawyers, and campaign consultants. And over the next ten years, Father Arne, as he was known to one and all, became a singularly winsome and effective witness to Christ and an exceptionally dynamic builder of Christian community.

His many friends and admirers, a "great cloud of witnesses" among whom I was honored to be numbered, had expected Father Arne to be celebrating Easter 2017 from a different station in the communion of saints. A long, heroic, and uncomplaining battle with cancer seemed to be heading in the wrong direction earlier in the year, and we all imagined that, as we watched the Easter fire being lit and were blessed with Easter water, Father Arne would be keeping an eye on us from the Throne of Grace.

But good medical care and his own resolve to keep bearing witness as long as possible beat the lugubrious oddsmakers of February, such that Father Arne was able to celebrate a last Easter, in anticipation of the eternal Easter that awaited him, and to which he was called a few months later. Those who loved him and shared his faith knew that, at his death, it was less a matter of losing a friend than of gaining an intercessor.

There was a lot of talk in Father Arne's last years about a "Benedict Option", and while no one seems to know precisely what that might mean, the Ben-Op, at least as advertised, does suggest a certain withdrawal from public life for the sake of forming intentional communities of character. Yet any notion that Saint Benedict's monasteries opted out of the life and culture of their times is mistaken. Benedictine monasteries were crucial in preserving the cultural memory of the West during the so-called Dark Ages, and over time they became centers of learning and scholarship, prayer and work that were instrumental in building the civilization of the High Middle Ages. Thus the better historical image for Christianity in postmodern America (and elsewhere in the West) is a "Gregorian Option": building or strengthening intentional communities of character as launchpads for witness, mission, and evangelization—just as Pope Saint Gregory the Great sent the man we now know as Saint Augustine of Canterbury to evangelize heathen England, and did so from the Benedictine monastery that Gregory had founded in Rome.

Catholics in the nation's capital may wish, however, to dub this alternative the "Panula Option". For in addition to directing an exceptional Catholic bookstore and chapel where Mass, confession, and spiritual direction were available (and popular), Father Arne Panula launched a "Leonine Forum" program at CIC. It gives several dozen up-and-coming young Washingtonians an intense introduction to Catholic social doctrine and an experience of Christian fellowship and service before sending them out to be Easter witnesses—in the White House, on Capitol Hill, in top-drawer law firms, and in the rest of often smugly secular Washington. The Forum's 2017 class included 38 "Leonine Fellows" selected from more than 140 applicants—a sure sign that the word was spreading that this program, named in honor of Pope Leo XIII, founding father of modern Catholic social doctrine, is Something Special.

And it was all because of Father Arne Panula and the fine staff he built at CIC over a decade of a remarkably effective ministry. During that time, Father Arne became, for many, the embodiment of what Saint John Paul II called the "New Evangelization" in the nation's capital. He could do that because, like the witnesses the Church reads about during Easter Week, he had met the Risen Lord. And that made all the difference.

An American Original
Robert Pickus (1923–2016)

I'm occasionally asked why I, a card-carrying member of the Guild of Public Intellectuals, never pursued doctoral studies. The short answer is that I met Robert Pickus, who was my personal doctoral program: a volcano of ideas who taught me more than I could possibly have absorbed from any number of courses, seminars, and dissertations, and who introduced me to a host of thinkers, including Midge Decter, Irving Kristol, Seymour Martin Lipset, and Norman Podhoretz, who, along with Richard John Neuhaus and Michael Novak, completed whatever in my education Pickus had left unfinished. When he died on January 22, 2016, at the age of ninety-two, I lost a friend and mentor who left an indelible imprint on my life, and the United States lost one of its most passionately patriotic citizens, a genuine American original.

The son of Belarussian immigrants and a veteran of OSS operations in England and Sweden during World War II, Pick, as he was universally known, spent the immediate postwar years studying political theory at the University of Chicago during that institution's glory days. Leaving Chicago with his doctoral coursework completed but "ABD" (all-but-dissertation, as the academic argot had it), he plunged into work for the American Friends Service Committee (AFSC); there, he coauthored *Speak Truth to Power*, a proposal for a peace-oriented U.S. foreign policy that drew the respect, if not the agreement, of George F. Kennan and Reinhold Niebuhr. But as the AFSC, like the rest of the peace movement, took a sharp left turn in the early 1960s, Pick became a sign of contradiction within—indeed, a target of seriously nasty obloquy from—the movement to which he had dedicated his professional life. For in Pickus' view, what called itself a "peace movement" became, in the early Vietnam years, an anti-American-power-in-the-world movement.

Part of that judgment was based on Pick's profound intellectual, moral, and political disdain for communism, which he knew to be a god that failed long before others figured that out. But the deeper root of his critique of the peace movement of his day was his love for the United States, which, for this scion of the great Eastern European Jewish migration to America, was the model of the kind of pluralistic, tolerant, democratic political community to which the world should aspire. The peace-movement people who spelled their country's name "Amerika" struck Robert Pickus, who proudly called himself a peace activist for more than a half-century, as moral idiots and dangerous fools. If the "Amerika" people (and the liberal fellow travelers who declined to criticize them, on the principle of *pas d'ennemis à gauche*) couldn't understand, and appreciate, how democratic politics and the rule of law made pluralist political community possible in the United States, how were those people going to contribute in any useful way to building a world in which law and politics replaced mass violence as the means of adjudicating conflict?

They weren't. And Pickus did not hesitate to tell them so, perhaps most memorably on May 21, 1965, "Vietnam Day" in Berkeley, California. For hours, the usual suspects, including Staughton Lynd and Jerry Rubin, had been saying the usual things the usual suspects said in those days; then it was Pick's turn to speak. He spoke as the Western-area director of an organization called Turn Toward Peace and an opponent of American policy in Vietnam. But he also spoke as a man who knew that Vietnamese communists, be they North Vietnamese or Viet Cong, were not agrarian reformers but totalitarians with blood on their hands. And he proceeded to tell the Berkeley crowd that their tacit, or in some cases explicit, support for the communist cause in Vietnam was a disgrace to anything that styled itself a "peace" movement.

Five minutes into his speech, he said that much of what he had heard thus far had been "Cold War clichés—only they're not American Cold War clichés; they're the clichés of the communist world". Then he switched his attention, from the faculty who had already spoken to the students they'd harangued. What he could not understand, he said, was "why so many bright people [have] accepted so much pure crap (that was worn out thirty years ago) as though it was really a way to stand for what you really want: resistance to the whole idea of hatred, resistance to the idea of violence, resistance to the idea of exploitation. And yet what takes place here? Staughton Lynd stands up and talks about [how] annihilation in a Brooks Brothers suit is still murder, and I don't hear anybody ... talking about the fact that murder at the point of a Viet Cong knife is also 'still murder'." It was impossible, he continued, to talk sensibly about a peace process in Vietnam that resulted in governments based on a "belief in the dignity of the individual man" if you "are caught in what ... I will now accurately describe: in hatred." Hatred, that is, of America and its role in the world.

It was about time, he said, that America "got rid of all the McCarthyite crap". But he was also "sick and tired of a reverse McCarthyism masquerading as an argument for freedom" by "applying the term 'red-baiting' to anyone who wants to talk about communist politics and what's wrong with them". And he then challenged students and faculty alike to think beyond the tired oversimplifications of "withdraw from Vietnam now" in order to face some serious questions: "Why are you withdrawing, to what end? Are you withdrawing to aid in achieving a stable settlement there? Do you want to see an international presence there that will guarantee that the opposition [to North Vietnam and the Viet Cong] will not be murdered?" The children of American privilege, studying at a great public institution of higher learning like Berkeley, ought to be able to manage something beyond "this idiotic isolationist line" of a "simple 'get out of Vietnam'". What Berkeley needed, he concluded, was "a lot more realistic pacifists and a lot fewer patsies" who took the bait and thought that "withdraw now" was the gutsy call. Let the Leftists he was criticizing "have your guts; I want your brains".

That final challenge bespoke the essence of Robert Pickus, who, for all that he devoted his life to peace activism in his singular (and noble) definition of it, was at bottom a teacher. The gang that organized Vietnam Day in Berkeley in May 1965 may have been drawn from the Tenured Faculty Subdivision of the Invincibly Ignorant; that much, at least, is suggested by their refusal to print his speech along with the many others delivered that day. But over fifty years of leading organizations variously known as Acts for Peace, Turn Toward Peace, the World Without War Council, and the James Madison Foundation, Pick's tutelage left a deep imprint on many minds and souls, including mine.

It was Pick, a son of Judaism, who reminded me, a Catholic, that, since the days of Augustine, Catholicism had thought of peace as the product of law and politics: in Augustine's fine phrase, peace is *tranquillitas ordinis*, the "tranquillity of order". (I let Pick talk me into making that piece of Latin the title of my first major book, an error I did not repeat in future works.)

It was Pick, a pacifist, who showed me, a Catholic theologian committed to the just-war tradition, how these two moral commitments could work together when "work for peace" was not traduced to agitation against alleged American "militarism", but focused on finding legal and political alternatives to war in resolving international conflict.

It was Pick who, by insisting that peace and freedom were inseparable, helped me to think about "human rights" in a disciplined, precise way, and who first showed me what John Paul II and Václav Havel later confirmed: that the robust defense of human rights behind the Iron Curtain was one crucial key to bringing down the Berlin Wall and liberating what Pickus understood full well were "captive nations".

But the deeper lesson Pick taught was about the difference between "career" and "vocation". There was nothing wrong with a career. But to live vocationally, in service of a great cause, was something noble and soul-strengthening. In his case, that meant the vocation to advance the prospects of a world in which, as Albert Camus (one of his heroes) put it, we were "neither victims nor executioners". I joined him in pursuing that vocation for nine years; but he understood that, when a parallel vocational call came to me in 1989 in the offer of the presidency of the Ethics and Public Policy Center, it was a call I ought to answer.

To the end, he believed in building what he often called an "American peace effort worthy of the name"—one that firmly rejected all forms of tyranny, especially the communist variety; one that cherished American democracy and saw American political, economic, and, yes, military power as essential in moving the world toward a greater measure of political community; one that understood that this is an imperfect world, in which utopian politics too often turns into a tacit acquiescence in evil—or evil itself; one that honored the rule of law and wasn't seduced by leftist revolutionary violence; one that acknowledged the present incompetencies and corruptions of international organizations while working to reform them.

He was an American original, this pacifist who admired Ronald Reagan. And if he was all too frequently defeated in the great battle of his life—the battle to prevent what styled itself the American peace movement from becoming captive to what he regarded as infantile anti-Americanism—he never stopped trying. For in the trying, he was living vocationally, in response to what he understood to be the deep moral truths embodied in the Jewish Scriptures and the great Western tradition of political philosophy.

Cosmic Traveler
Pioneer 10 (1972–)

In late April 1983, a small, 571-pound spacecraft, Pioneer 10, whirred past Pluto and headed out of the solar system into the immensity of interstellar space. Launched by an Atlas-Centaur rocket from Cape Canaveral in 1972, Pioneer 10 continued to function long and far beyond its builders' expectations; even as it exited the solar system, it sent back radio signals to its terrestrial home, signals from such an extraordinary distance that it took them hours to complete their journey, even at the speed of light. In 2003, the electrical power needed for its radio transmissions was exhausted, and, some 7.5 billion miles from where its voyage began, Pioneer 10 was beyond the reach of those who first made it. But the Little Probe That Could did not stop. On and on it goes, and will go, a bottle with a message tossed into the infinite sea of space.

Biology-watcher Lewis Thomas once asked what message we should put out into the cosmos, on the assumption that there were ears (or something like ears) to hear it. "I would vote for Bach," wrote Thomas, "all of Bach, streamed out into space, over and over again. We would be bragging, of course, but it is surely excusable for us to put the best possible face on at the beginning of such an acquaintance. We can tell the harder truths later." The message in the bottle that is Pioneer 10 was more modest: a plate on the side of the spacecraft displays two drawings, of a man and a woman, and a schematic diagram of our planetary system, indicating the home from which the space traveler came. But why even bother with a message? Is there anyone out there listening?

Was the divine creativity, the Creator's zest for self-comprehending life, exhausted with our species? It may seem statistically improbable that ours is the only planet in the enormity of the cosmos on which the conditions for sentient life exist; but from another statistical point of view, the exquisitely fine calibrations that make life on

Earth possible may just be a one-off miracle, ultimately inspired by that zestful Creator. In any event, and unlike the makers (and some viewers) of *E. T.* and *Close Encounters of the Third Kind*, we should not be looking into the cosmos for an extraterrestrial redemption, a *deus ex machina* who will relieve us of the burden of our earthly responsibilities, or teach us things that we are perfectly capable of knowing on our own.

The meaning of Pioneer 10, though, is not exhausted if in fact we are alone, if there really is no one out there to decode our simple message in a bottle. For what Pioneer 10 reminds us, as we imagine this frail, man-made object sailing through the black sea of space, is that the stuff of the stars and the stuff of ourselves is the same stuff. Out of the same cosmic brew have come Douglas firs, blue crabs, silicon, diamonds, oxygen, DNA, Louisville Sluggers, black holes, stars in nova and stars being born—and us. It is a mind-boggling thought, in the literal sense of the term, comprehensible perhaps only at the outer reaches of higher mathematics and metaphysics. Now, with Pioneer 10 and its successors, like the New Horizons probe that mesmerized the world with its 2015 photos of a heart-shaped surface feature on Pluto, we have put something of ourselves back out into the cosmos: an act of science, to be sure, but in a curious way an act of faith as well.

The millions of Americans who read Tom Wolfe's bestseller, *The Right Stuff*, know that we went into space with mixed motives and that considerations of national prestige, military anxieties, and bureaucratic infighting had as much to do with the early space program as a Copernican thirst for understanding. Still, I wish we had kept going at the same pace as during the Apollo moon-landing project. Yes, the costs are considerable; and yes, there are lots of things to spend the money on here. But what is the price of a sense of adventurous purpose? How do you "cost out" the broadening of our horizons that would have come from a manned exploration of the planets? Can the value of that incredible "Earthrise" photograph taken by Apollo 8 astronaut William Anders at Christmas 1968—a blue-green orb suspended in a dark ocean, so clearly a fragile-yet-glorious domicile that deserves our protection and nurture—be measured in dollar terms?

Human beings need a focus outside of themselves in order to bring our best elements to bear on the business of living. The space program has provided that kind of horizon for human achievement and understanding. It was a horizon that, as a boy, I had hoped to be able to explore personally. In the early 1980s, I was walking along the Washington State coast on a crystalline spring night when the sky seemed carpeted with stars; and I suddenly felt a wave of sadness pass over me. I would never get out there. But someday we humans will, for we have no permanent home here—our sun will eventually burn out, and we must take our cosmic pilgrimage elsewhere. That's a long time off, thank God. For the moment, it is reassuring to know that a work of our hands is blazing a path for us—and that a merciful God may allow us to spend some portion of eternal life in (as *Star Trek* used to put it) going "where no man has gone before".

So, safe travels, Pioneer 10. You carry a little piece of us all out into the vastness of the cosmos.

Ferocity, Courage, and Grace

Frank Robinson (1935–2019)

Hard as it may be for those who know them only from their twenty-first-century woes, the Baltimore Orioles won more games than any other team in baseball's major leagues for almost a quarter-century, from 1960 to 1983, the year of their last world championship.

The driver of that remarkable success was something called the "Oriole Way", several lifetimes of baseball experience distilled into a written manual of instructions on Playing the Game Right that the organization began drilling into its rookie free agents and draftees in Bluefield, West Virginia, at the bottom-of-the-barrel Appalachian League, and continued inculcating up to and through the major-league level. The Oriole Way, stressing pitching, defense, and situational awareness, built a cadre of players who were often more than the sum of their individual skills and thereby won more than their share of games. But something else was needed to turn routine competitiveness into four World Series appearances in six years. That human pivot in Baltimore's baseball fortunes was the greatest player I ever saw bend games to his will: Frank Robinson.

In 1964 and 1965, the Orioles challenged for the American League pennant but couldn't seem to get over the last hurdle. Then, over the winter of 1965–1966, Orioles general manager Harry Dalton pulled off one of the great trades in baseball history, acquiring Frank Robinson from the Cincinnati Reds for pitchers Milt Pappas, Dick Simpson, and Jack Baldschun. Trying to justify the trade, and much to his subsequent embarrassment, Reds general manager Bill DeWitt described Robinson (who had been voted Most Valuable Player of the National League in 1961) as an "old thirty".

Right.

When twenty-year-old Jim Palmer heard the ball explode off Frank Robinson's bat on the first day of spring training in 1966, he turned to the others standing around the batting cage and said,

"We just won the American League." Which the Orioles did in a cakewalk, with the man everyone called, simply, "Frank" leading the charge from Opening Day on—and punctuating the season by hitting the first and only home run ever driven completely out of old Memorial Stadium. (The point of its exit was subsequently marked by an orange-and-black flag emblazoned with one word: HERE.) Motivated in part, one suspects, by resentment over Bill DeWitt's geriatric putdown, but even more by his own innate and fierce competitiveness, Frank Robinson had his second MVP season in 1966, while winning batting's triple crown (the league leadership in batting average [.316], home runs [49], and runs batted in [122]) and leading the Orioles to a four-game sweep of the Los Angeles Dodgers in the World Series.

I was sitting behind first base in Memorial Stadium with my grandfather Weigel during the fourth game. And in my mind's eye I can still see a glaring Frank Robinson digging in against another intimidator, brushback artist Don Drysdale—and then hitting a lightning bolt of a line drive into the left-field bleachers (a dozen rows or so beneath the HERE flag) to give the Birds both their margin of victory and the world championship. One can only imagine what Bill DeWitt was thinking.

Baltimore had seen baseball excellence before, not least in the other immortal Robinson of that era, Brooks, he of the miracle-making glove at third base. But none of us had ever seen anyone quite like Number 20. On stepping into the batter's box, Frank would deliberately erase its chalk back line, plant the back edge of his right foot an inch or two behind where the line had been in order to get a millisecond longer to look at the pitch, and lean over the plate as if daring the pitcher to come inside. And from that hunched position, rockets were launched—or perhaps howitzer shots would be the better metaphor, because, as Jim Palmer had quickly detected, nothing ever sounded as instantaneously explosive as a baseball coming off Frank Robinson's bat.

He was also a demon on the basepaths and a singularly graceful (and fearless) outfielder—on one occasion tumbling into the stands at the original, pre-Steinbrenner Yankee Stadium and fighting the Evil Empire's fans for the ball he had caught while tumbling backwards over the low right-field wall in The House That Ruth Built. Beyond all that, he was the team's undisputed leader, presiding in a periwig (adopted from a mop) over the Orioles' postgame kangaroo court, where in-game foul-ups were mercilessly prosecuted and fined. It was keep-everybody-loose locker-room buffoonery, but it also sent the subtle message to the other twenty-four men on the team: excellence was expected of everyone, not just the team's stars.

To watch Frank Robinson in his prime was to watch a man of exceptional physical gifts and considerable athletic courage. What remains most powerfully ingrained in the memory, however, is that indomitable will to prevail. It was fearsome and awesome and, in its own way, a beautiful thing: a ferocity of purpose, rooted in character, that calls to mind the tribute paid by Leo Durocher to yet another Robinson, the Brooklyn Dodgers' legendary Jackie. Jackie Robinson and Leo the Lip had a contentious relationship that included verbal bench-jockeying that would singe the ears of fans (and give the PC press the vapors) today. In summing up Robinson, the Dodgers' Number 42, however, Durocher painted a parallel portrait of Robinson, the Orioles' Number 20: "Ya want a guy that comes to play. This guy didn't just come to play. He come to beat ya. He come to shove the [expletive deleted] bat right up your [use your imagination]."

Inelegant? Perhaps. Awe-inspiring? To be sure.

There is another facet of Frank Robinson's playing time in Baltimore, which ran from 1966 through 1971 and is memorialized on his plaque in the National Baseball Hall of Fame, that should be remembered.

The Baltimore of my youth was a segregated city, psychologically and emotionally as well as legally. The human barriers began to break down in the late 1950s, when the great Baltimore Colts teams led by John Unitas and Gino Marchetti featured high-quality African American players such as Lenny Moore, Gene "Big Daddy" Lipscomb, and Jim Parker. I remain convinced, though, that the real breakthrough from the old shibboleths and prejudices began in 1966, when Frank Robinson arrived on a Baltimore team whose undisputed star was that other Robinson, Brooks, a white Southerner who had grown up in Little Rock, Arkansas, in the days when the U.S. Army came to town to enforce the Supreme Court's desegregation decision in *Brown v. Board of Education.*

It could have been tense. It wasn't. Brooks, the classic gentleman who had been American League MVP in 1964, and Frank, the
fiery rebel against convention who would later break a color line
and become MLB's first African American manager, quickly became friends and allies, even kidding each other and the press about
then-standard racial stereotypes and taboos. (If memory serves, Frank
once deflected an impertinent reporter's question about clubhouse
etiquette by saying that Brooks could borrow his used shower tow-
els whenever he wanted; Brooks howled in laughter.) Moreover,
Brooks' acknowledgment of Frank's kangaroo-court leadership sent
a signal to any malcontent or bigot tempted to resent the fact that the
new team leader was a proudly black man: insubordination was out
of the question.

These two men—one a titanic Beethoven, the other a graceful
Haydn—set an example of unity in diversity in the pursuit of common goals from which Baltimore (and the rest of America, for that
matter) is still trying to learn.

It seems somehow inappropriate to wish, for the late, great Frank
Robinson, *requiescat in pace*. He was too ferocious a competitor to
imagine him quiescent, even postmortem. The peace he richly
deserves, however, is that noble peace that comes on the far side of
striving and struggle, and at the end of a life lived for the excellence
he singularly embodied, for me and many others.

The Pioneer

Jackie Robinson (1919–1972)

In the history of the modern American civil rights movement, three iconic moments are typically cited.

- May 17, 1954: The U.S. Supreme Court hands down its decision in *Brown v. Board of Education of Topeka*, declaring segregated— "separate but equal"—public schools unconstitutional.
- August 28, 1963: Two hundred thousand Americans participate in the March on Washington and hear Martin Luther King, Jr., proclaim his dream of a country in which his children will be judged by the content of their character rather than the color of their skin; ten months later, Congress enacts the 1964 Civil Rights Act.
- March 3, 1965: Civil rights marchers are assaulted by police tear gas and billy clubs on the Edmund Pettis Bridge in Selma, Alabama; five months later, President Lyndon B. Johnson signs into law the Voting Rights Act, vindicating the Selma marchers' cause.

These were noble moments, worth remembering; I certainly cherish my memories of encounters with Bayard Rustin, who organized the march that made Dr. King a national eminence. Yet I also believe there was a fourth iconic moment in America's journey from a land fouled by segregation to the most racially egalitarian nation on the planet. The man at the center of that fourth dramatic moment was an American legend whose accomplishments should rank as high as anyone's in the pantheon of civil rights heroes.

On April 15, 1947, the Brooklyn Dodgers opened their National League season against the Boston Braves at Ebbets Field. The Dodger first baseman that day was Jackie Robinson: the first African American to play in a major-league game since the infamous "color line" was drawn in the 1880s. At UCLA in 1939–1941, Robinson was perhaps the greatest amateur athlete in the country, a star in track-and-field, football, and basketball. After service as an Army officer in World War II, he was playing shortstop for the Kansas City Monarchs of the Negro American League when he was signed to a minor-league contract by "The Mahatma", Branch Rickey, a cigar-chomping Methodist and the Dodgers' general manager. Rickey was determined to break the color line, and he deliberately chose Jack Roosevelt Robinson to do so.

And not because Jackie Robinson was a mild-mannered wall-flower, but precisely because he was a warrior who played with a fierce determination to prevail. Robinson was to be a warrior with a difference, however: Rickey, an adept psychologist who believed in the essential fairness of the American people, wanted a man with the courage *not* to fight back against the racist slurs, beanballs, and spikings that were sure to come his way—except by giving an unforgettable performance on the field.

Which is what Jackie Robinson, the immortal Number 42, delivered. Grainy black-and-white videos today remind us of a truth that the baseball world learned in 1947: there has never been anything more exciting in baseball, including the majestic home run and the overpowering no-hitter, than 42 stealing a base, especially home. Rather than hollering back at bigots during his rookie year, Robinson beat them with a slashing, attacking style of baseball that helped lift the Dodgers to the National League pennant and brought them within one game of a World Series victory over the lordly Yankees (who didn't sign an African American player until Elston Howard in 1955).

It was a performance for the ages. And it changed America.

In this entertainment-saturated twenty-first century, it may be hard to recall the grip that baseball had on the national emotions and imagination in 1947. But as the late Columbia University cultural historian Jacques Barzun (an immigrant from France) used to say, whoever wants to understand the heart and mind of America had better understand baseball. On April 14, 1947, that nation-defining pastime still embodied the nation's original sin. The next day, Jackie Robinson began to accelerate a change in America's heart and mind. That change made possible *Brown v. Board of Education*, the Civil Rights Act, and the Voting Rights Act.

As his first game in the majors fades ever farther into the past, and tawdry hucksters of various ideological persuasions try to turn race-baiting into political capital, America desperately needs the example of Jackie Robinson, to whom the country owes an enormous round of applause and a prayer for the repose of a noble soul.

The Paradoxical Peacemaker
Anwar Sadat (1918–1981)

If the mark of a great teacher is the ability to tell imaginative stories that illuminate complicated realities, then Patrick Morgan, who was teaching at Washington State University in the days when I knew him, certainly qualified as a great teacher. In his courses on national security in the late 1970s and early 1980s, Pat was confronted, regularly, with the charge that all this Soviet-American arms race business was just madness. At which point Morgan auctioned off a dollar bill—and got $1.80 for it.

The rules were simple. Professor Morgan announced that he had a dollar bill to auction: the highest bidder won and the second highest bidder had to pay Morgan his last bid. The bidding started at ten cents and worked its way up in increments of ten cents. Pretty soon the bidding was at ninety cents, and while the winner wouldn't get a great deal, he'd at least win ten cents. But now the guy in second place is very nervous; he's going to lose eighty cents. So he bids a dollar; he won't win anything, but he won't lose, either. But now the guy at ninety cents can't afford to stop, so he has to bid $1.10. He'll lose ten cents in any event, but that's better than losing ninety cents. And so it goes, on and on.

I thought about Pat Morgan's dollar bill auction when Anwar Sadat was assassinated on October 6, 1981—not so much because Sadat was a gambler, but because Sadat knew that the game of politics wasn't madness if you found yourself in the middle of it and took your responsibilities as a national leader seriously. You could curse the darkness and damn the madness, but it wouldn't make any difference. If you wanted to break out of the cycle of bidding $1.80 for $1, you had to change the rules of the game—and in such a way that neither you nor your opponent lost, but only gained.

Sadat changed the rules of the particular game in which he was caught—the seemingly insoluble conflict between Egypt and Israel—

in a fundamental way. His step off an Egyptian plane and onto the tarmac at Jerusalem's Ben-Gurion Airport was arguably the single most electrifying moment in international politics between V-J Day and the Fall of the Berlin Wall—electrifying because it captured the simple human yearning for peace to which so many leaders pay lip service and which so few are able to achieve.

Sadat's greatness as a peacemaker was multilayered. He understood that statecraft is soulcraft and that symbolic acts, if they're genuine expressions of political will, can be more powerful than any piece of military hardware. Sadat also understood the limits of traditional diplomacy. He knew that one had to risk: one had to act, prior to agreement with an adversary, in ways that made agreement with him more likely. The stagnant variables of the accepted game could not be left alone if they were the primary obstacles to agreement.

But those who would take Anwar Sadat as a model peacemaker need to confront the whole measure of the man. Sadat did not die in the white tie and cutaway of the Nobel laureate; he died in a field marshal's uniform. His last sight on earth was not of swords beaten into plowshares, but of "his children", the Egyptian Army on parade—and a parade celebrating the beginning of the Yom Kippur War, which in Sadat's mind had given him the political leverage to make peace with Israel. One need not think him infallible to understand that, in Mohammad Anwar el-Sadat, the world had a consummate political leader—one who was able to gather his people for new departures, who recognized the "appointed time" and seized it, who could hold two ideas, "security" and "peace", together in his head at once. In doing so, Sadat exemplified Harold Nicholson's judgment that "the best kind of diplomat is a humane skeptic".

When Sadat was a major figure on the world stage in the 1970s and early 1980s, many of those most vocal about peace, in Western Europe and in America, were skeptical about very little, and least of all about their own moral and political rectitude. They were enthusiasts with the enthusiast's typical intolerance for ambiguity, for the vast gray area that is politics, and especially international politics. Sadat's life, and the manner of his death, should have given these people pause—and it should continue to give pause, decades later. In the days after he was murdered by Islamist fanatics who imagined that they were obeying the will of God by obeying a fatwa issued by the blind sheikh, Omar Abdel-Rahman, it was fashionable in the media to speak of Sadat's contradictions, or, more kindly, the ironies, of his life. Neither of these genteel epithets made much sense. That Sadat, the man of peace, died in uniform was neither contradictory nor ironic: it was an expression of the tension in which real leadership, committed to peace yet understanding the realities of power, lives.

In an interview some weeks before his murder, Anwar Sadat, whose later years as Egyptian president were marked by controversies and threats, said that "I will not die one hour before God decides that it is time for me to die." Those who want to walk his way of trenchant peacemaking might ponder the circumstances in which God decided that Anwar Sadat should die.

The Old-School Jesuit
James V. Schall, S.J. (1928–2019)

The most distinguished son of Pocahontas, Iowa, Father James V. Schall, S.J., died at age ninety-one on April 17, 2019, just as Lent was drawing to a close and Easter was visible on the horizon. That he was thus able to celebrate the Paschal Mystery at the Throne of Grace was entirely appropriate.

Father Schall was what's usually referred to as an "old-school Jesuit"—meaning (to my mind) that he was the kind of Jesuit that Saint Ignatius Loyola imagined when he founded the Society of Jesus in the sixteenth century. Jim Schall was both a man of rock-solid Catholic faith and a first-rate intellectual, a distinguished political philosopher at home with political theory from Plato through the moderns. His faith informed his intellectual work, as his intellect refined his faith. He was an exceptionally gifted teacher; just before he was put out to pasture by Jesuit superiors who didn't seem to grasp that he was a magnet for the kind of students they ought to be recruiting, his last lecture at Georgetown University was attended by hundreds, who spilled out of venerable Gaston Hall into the surrounding corridors. He was a devoted priest, a masterful spiritual director, and a counselor who encouraged his students to think vocationally, whether about the priesthood or consecrated religious life, marriage, or their professional careers.

He was also an ascetic, whom self-denial, religious disciplines, and—in his last years—illness had whittled down, so that in his ninth decade he looked like something chiseled out of tough, hardened wood: a lean, mean pirate in a Roman collar (which he always wore). But there was no meanness in the man, only a sweetness of temperament wed to a bracing, unblinking honesty about the state of the Church, the world, and the Society to which he had given his life. His suffering from cancer, his being blinded in one eye, and his increasing deafness did make his legion of friends and protégés (including the Georgetown alumni who proudly claimed to have "majored in Schall") wonder about God's ways with his most devoted servants; Father Schall would have said that suffering is good for you, because if you conform your sufferings to those of Christ in his Passion, then God's grace helps you grow through suffering into the imitation of Christ that every Christian should be.

Jim Schall's life and holy death invite a reflection on the gamble that the Catholic Church took when, during the cultural tsunami of the sundry Protestant Reformations, it approved Saint Ignatius' proposal to create an elite corps of priestly guerrillas, formed by his *Spiritual Exercises*, whom Ignatius would deploy to "set the world ablaze", as the inscription on the base of his statue at Jesuit GHQ in Rome reminds us. As my friend Russell Hittinger once put it with his usual flair, the *Exercises* were "a spirituality invented for European intellectuals paddling canoes up rivers in the middle of nowhere", surrounded by what were then known as "savages". The *Exercises* were thus very much a me-and-God affair; the gamble was that such intense interiority would not lead to a radical, delusory subjectivism, because a well-formed Jesuit would also be unshakeable in his commitment to the truth of Catholic faith and unbreakably bound to the teaching authority of the Church. Cut that tether to truth and ecclesiastical authority, and trouble would begin.

And then there was that quite deliberate Ignatian elitism. Self-defined, self-constructed, and self-perpetuated elites are almost always trouble within a complex institution. They risk becoming what C. S. Lewis called an "Inner Ring", which imagines itself composed of superior types to whom others must defer, and who are, because of their superiority, absolved from some of the myriad loyalties that bind others to the institution. The Jesuits' stern, unbending fidelity—embodied in their famous fourth vow and its promise of radical obedience to the pope and radical availability for any mission the pope decreed—would, it was hoped, prevent this elite corps from decomposing into something akin to its own Church, marching to the beat of its own, self-consciously superior beat.

The Church's gamble paid off in the life of men such as Father Jim Schall, for whom radical commitment to the full symphony of Catholic truth was liberating rather than confining—especially when that commitment was intellectually refined by a lifelong immersion in the great books of Western civilization. Whether that gamble has paid off in respect of the entire Society of Jesus as the Catholic Church experiences it in the twenty-first century is a question that caused Father Schall more than a little anxiety over the course of his long life.

In addition to his asceticism, his brilliance, and that unfailing twinkle in his (remaining) eye, Father Schall was an attractive and compelling human personality—and a great teacher and mentor—because, while he took the spiritual life and the life of the mind with great seriousness, he never took himself seriously. Thus he could poke gentle fun at intellectual life, at its best and at its contemporary worst, with a book whose double-barreled subtitle alone ought to have won Schall a National Book Award: *Another Sort of Learning: Selected Contrary Essays on How Finally to Acquire an Education While Still in College or Anywhere Else—Containing Some Belated Advice about How to Employ Your Leisure Time When Ultimate Questions Remain Perplexing in Spite of Your Highest Earned Academic Degree, Together with Sundry Book Lists Nowhere Else in Captivity to Be Found.*

The years from 2002 on have been tough for Catholic priests in the United States, whose reputation as a group is being damaged by revelations of the perfidy of some 4 percent of their number. From his present station in the communion of saints, I am confident that my friend Father Jim Schall, a priest to the core whose priesthood was indeed an icon of the eternal priesthood of Jesus Christ, is interceding for priests, for the reform of the Church, and for the reform of the Society of which he was an exemplary, if too often unappreciated, member. Thank you, Jim, for being a true man for others. Thank you for your tireless example of priestly holiness and intellectual integrity.

Requiescat in pace.

The Truth about Conscience
Sophie Scholl (1921–1943)

On February 22, 1943, Sophie and Hans Scholl and their friend Christian Probst were executed by guillotine at Munich's Stadelheim Prison for the crime of high treason, having been convicted in the notorious "People's Court" presided over by Nazi ideologue Roland Freisler. What had they done? They were the leaders of an anti-Nazi student organization, the White Rose, and they had been caught distributing leaflets at their university in the Bavarian capital; the leaflets condemned the Third Reich, its genocide of the Jews, and its futile war.

How did young people once active in the Hitler Youth come to recognize the evil of the Nazi regime and risk their lives to oppose it?

The 2005 Oscar-nominated film *Sophie Scholl: The Final Days* offers part of the answer. The garish brutality of the Nazis, not least at its Nuremberg party rallies, was a first hint to serious young people that something was seriously wrong here. The White Rose youngsters were also thinkers who studied Socrates, Plato, and Pascal under the tutelage of Kurt Huber, a philosophy professor who despised the Hitler regime. The leaflets that were their primary resistance tool included references to Goethe, Aristotle, Schiller, and Lao Tzu—further signs of deep and broad reading.

What you won't learn from the film, however, is that the triggering inspiration for their activism was the "Lion of Münster", Archbishop Clemens von Galen, whose anti-Nazi preaching convinced the members of the White Rose that reading, study, and discussion must eventually lead to action in circumstances of grave evil. So, between June 1942 and February 1943, the White Rose produced and distributed six leaflets urging others to nonviolent resistance against the Nazi regime. To stand by silently, they claimed, was to be complicit in "the most horrible of crimes—crimes that infinitely outdistance every human measure". To do nothing was to truckle to Hitler; and "every word that comes from Hitler's mouth is a lie."

The fourth pamphlet made a promise: "We will not be silent. We are your bad conscience. The White Rose will not leave you in peace!" And therein lies a clue to another inspiration for the Scholls and their friends: John Henry Newman and his writings on conscience.

In a 2018 article in Britain's *Catholic Herald*, Paul Shrimpton noted that the youngsters of the White Rose were deeply influenced by Augustine's *Confessions* and Georges Bernanos' *Diary of a Country Priest*. But it was Newman's sermons, recommended to the White Rose students by a philosopher who had converted to Catholicism after reading Newman's *Grammar of Assent*, which prompted that fourth pamphlet with its call to heed the demanding voice of conscience.

Shrimpton reports that when Sophie Scholl's boyfriend, Fritz Hartnagel, was sent by the Wehrmacht to the Russian front in 1942, Sophie gave him two volumes of Newman's sermons. He later wrote her that "we know by whom we are created, and that we stand in a relationship of moral obligation to our creator. Conscience gives us the capacity to distinguish between good and evil"—words, Shrimpton observed, that "were taken almost verbatim from a famous sermon of Newman's called 'The Testimony of Conscience'". On the witness stand before the odious Judge Freisler (who died in 1945 at the business end of a U.S. Army Air Force bomb), twenty-one-year-old Sophie Scholl testified that it was her conscience, and her Christian conviction, that had led her to nonviolent resistance against Hitler and his gangsters. That Christian conscience, we now know, was formed in part by a serious intellectual and spiritual encounter with Saint John Henry Newman.

There is a lot of talk in twenty-first-century Catholicism about conscience, and Newman is invoked by many prominent personalities in those debates. So it might be useful for all concerned, including Church leaders in Munich, where the White Rose youngsters gave their lives for the truth, to ponder Newman's influence on these contemporary martyrs.

What did the members of the White Rose learn from Newman about conscience? They learned that conscience could not be ignored or manipulated. They learned that the voice of God speaking through our consciences sets before us what is life-giving and what is death-dealing. They learned that conscience can be stern, but that in submitting to the truths it conveys, we are liberated in the deepest meaning of human freedom.

They learned that obedience to conscience can make us courageous, and that to strive to live an ideal with the help of grace is to live a truly noble life with an undivided heart.

He Had a Hammer (and Sickle)
Pete Seeger (1919–2014)

Pete Seeger died on January 27, 2014, rich in years (ninety-four) and honors (a lifetime-achievement Grammy and the National Medal of Arts). His death rated a segment on the *PBS News Hour,* during which the inconvenient fact that Seeger had been a member of the U.S. Communist Party for years was finessed by the expedient of noting that he had eventually left the party. What Pete Seeger never left, of course, was the Left—not the pragmatic liberal world of Harry Truman, John F. Kennedy, Hubert Humphrey, and Scoop Jackson, but the hard left that created Stalin's Popular Front in the 1930s and that spelled the country's name "Amerika" in the Sixties.

With songs like "Where Have All the Flowers Gone?", "If I Had a Hammer", and "Turn, Turn, Turn" (best performed, if I may say, by the Byrds), Seeger did as much as anyone to popularize the folk music renaissance of the late Fifties and early Sixties. But the adulation that came Seeger's way in the latter decades of his life had less to do with his mastery of the five-string banjo and his songwriting than with his status in certain circles as a living martyr: the man who stiffed the House Un-American Activities Committee (HUAC), found himself blacklisted, and was reduced to performing on college campuses for a while.

Blacklisting is obviously bad business. What struck me at Seeger's death, however, was that the ugly habit of blacklisting had migrated on the political spectrum. Ask a lot of people the first thing they think of when they hear "blacklist", and the response will likely be "Joe McCarthy" or "HUAC". The proper response would be "Andrew Cuomo".

In mid-January 2014, just before Seeger left this vale of tears to meet Karl Marx, the New York governor indulged himself in a remarkable screed on a local radio station. His principal vexation was the "gridlock" in Washington that, on his account, was caused by "extreme Republicans", whom he distinguished from "moderate Republicans" (i.e., Republicans who tend to do what Andrew Cuomo wants them to do). Then, turning to his own Empire State, he announced that such extremists, among whom he listed "right-to-life" people, "have no place in the State of New York".

My professional obligations take me to New York with some frequency; and despite Cuomo's rant, I somehow doubt that there will be immigration-and-customs agents at Penn Station checking to see if I am one of those deplorable right-to-lifers before I detrain and begin contributing to New York's exchequer by paying its exorbitant state sales tax on various goods and services. Still, it's instructive to know that, by the lights of its fifty-sixth governor, I am in New York on sufferance—much like I was, I suppose, when I crossed into East Berlin in 1987 and was given a hard stare by the *Vopo* goon who examined my U.S. passport and looked at me as if I were a lower life-form. (I got a measure of payback by affixing a Baltimore Orioles sticker to a stancheon facing the East German side of the Brandenburg Gate—a calling card I also left in 1990 on the plate-glass window of the G.U.M. department store in Moscow, straight across from Lenin's Tomb.)

But back to the matter at hand. Andrew Cuomo is a blacklister—in the moral, if not literal, sense of the term. He deems unfit to live in his state those who disagree with his fervent, indeed fanatical, embrace of the most extreme form of the abortion license. Press him hard enough and he might even say such people are un-American. Thus the HUAC ethos—those who disagree are dangerously un-American—has been reconstituted in our time by the left-liberal governor of New York.

So it was not without a certain sense of ironies in the fire that I read Governor Cuomo's statement on the death of Pete Seeger, who waited until three years after the collapse of the Soviet Union to apologize "for once believing Stalin was just a hard driver", not the mass murderer that more honest and discerning men and women on the democratic left had known him to be a half-century earlier: the Pete Seeger who, according to the *motu proprio* from the gubernatorial *cathedra* in Albany, inspired Andrew Cuomo and, Cuomo hoped, others in their quest to "make New York State the progressive capital of the nation".

Where have all the liberals gone, long time passing? Not quite all have gone hard left. But Andrew Cuomo did, becoming a blacklister in the process. I'd like to say that Pete Seeger deserved better, and for his music, he did. But not for his politics.

The Best of a Troubling Clan
R. Sargent Shriver (1915–2011)

R. Sargent Shriver, who died on January 18, 2011, was the last of the classic American Catholic liberals. Advocate of racial justice when that took real courage; founding director of the Peace Corps and inspiration of a generation of Americans dedicated to serving the global poor; director of Lyndon Johnson's well-intended if ill-conceived domestic War on Poverty; ambassador to France and vice-presidential candidate, Shriver lived one of the richest of public lives, which included his partnership with his equally pro-life wife, Eunice Kennedy Shriver, in the Special Olympics movement.

We last met a few years before his death when Sarge called me up and invited me to lunch. He had read and liked my *Letters to a Young Catholic* and wanted me to sign Christmas gift copies for several of the younger members of the Shriver clan; I was happy to do so in his Special Olympics office, before we repaired across the street to the Willard Hotel for lunch. While I was signing, he casually and cheerfully mentioned that "lunch might be interesting, because I can't remember anything I've said ten minutes after I've said it." The Alzheimer's that finally killed him was already working its wicked ways, as his friendly warning indicated. Yet he was taking his condition with the equanimity that comes from deep faith, and from long experience with those battling various handicaps, physical and mental.

Lunch was utterly charming. I got Sarge to reminisce a bit about being an altar boy for Cardinal James Gibbons of Baltimore, who used to visit the Shriver's country place when Sarge was in short pants. He then changed the subject and asked me, "Where was I ambassador?" I said I thought his embassy had been to France, which he then described with gusto, remembering several run-ins with *Le Grand Charles* (de Gaulle). I didn't ask him about my favorite Shriver story, which involved him trying to be one of the boys at a steelworkers' bar in Johnstown, Pennsylvania, during the 1972 presidential campaign, when he was George McGovern's third-choice running mate. Sarge blew the gaffe by ordering "a Courvoisier; no, make it a double!" Still, I remember the strange, wonderful sense of being in the presence of a man who had not only made history in his own right but whose first American ancestor, David Shriver, had signed the Maryland Constitution and Bill of Rights in 1776.

Had his potential candidacy not been vetoed by his Kennedy in-laws, Sarge might have been President Johnson's vice-presidential running mate in 1964, a historical "what if" full of possibility: Shriver, as vice president or, later, president might have been able to connect the Democratic Party's civil rights commitments to a robust pro-life commitment, for Sarge knew in his heart that the pro-life cause was the logical, moral extension of the civil rights cause to which he had long dedicated himself. Instead, brother-in-law Ted Kennedy helped lead the Democratic Party into the pro-choice mania from which the party has never extricated itself, becoming far less inclusive and ever more strident in its defense of the indefensible.

Sarge and Eunice fought the good fight, but they never did the most dramatic thing they might have done for the pro-life cause, which was to leave the Democratic Party after the Clintonistas denied pro-life Pennsylvania Governor Bob Casey an opportunity to speak at the 1992 Democratic national convention. That was the break-point for many of us who had been lifelong, genetically programmed Democrats. That the Shrivers stayed put was a sadness; their departure would have sent shock waves through Democratic circles and might have provided an antidote to Mario Cuomo's "I'm personally opposed, but . . . ." mantra.

Had Sarge and Eunice Shriver prevailed over Ted Kennedy, the United States might not have developed, in the late twentieth century, something resembling a European-style two-party system, with a lifestyle-libertine, secularist party on the left contending against a quasi-Christian Democratic party on the right. America might have had two parties that understood that the right to life from conception until natural death is the first of "pre-political" human rights; indeed, it's the right whose acknowledgment makes a decent polity possible.

That was not to be. The country is the poorer for it.

Son-in-Law

Robert Charles Susil (1974–2010)

Four days after my son-in-law, Robert Susil, reentered Johns Hopkins Hospital, where he would die of an aggressive sarcoma on February 5, 2010, the Church marked the Feast of the Presentation of the Lord and read the gospel of Simeon's prophecy to Mary— that a "sword will pierce through your own soul" (Lk 2:35). That image of a sword, often described as a sword of sorrow, is the first of the traditional "seven dolors" of Our Lady of Sorrows, commemorated throughout the Church on September 15, the day after the Feast of the Triumph of the Cross. Yet if Our Lady is the first of disciples and the model of Christian discipleship, then the sword of sorrow must pass through each disciple's life, too, configuring us more closely to the Son from whose pierced side flowed blood, water, and the Church.

All of us who loved and esteemed Rob Susil were pierced by that sword before and after his death. He and my daughter Gwyneth had fought gallantly against his sarcoma since it was diagnosed in March 2008, with the able assistance of the entire Johns Hopkins medical family, of which Rob, as a specialist in radiation oncology completing his residency, was a valuable and beloved member. There are, however, things that even the best medicine cannot do, at even the greatest medical centers in the world. So those who loved Rob and shared his deep Catholic faith prayed for a miracle and were joined in that prayer by people all over the world. The miracle did not come; we know, however, that those prayers opened channels of grace and healing of which we are unaware, but for which we are grateful.

When Rob and Gwyneth first started seeing each other seriously, and after we were introduced, my wife said, "So, what do you think of Rob?" "Think?" I replied. "Smart, handsome, funny, 110 percent Catholic, loves Gwyneth, and likely to have an income. He's straight out of son-in-law Central Casting." He was so much more, though.

Rob was a brilliant young scientist, who held M.D. and Ph.D. degrees—and who didn't tell me that he had coauthored numerous scholarly articles until I saw the galley proofs of a forthcoming one when I was helping him and my daughter move into their first apartment.

He had a great appetite for learning; weakened by chemotherapy and anemia, he was nevertheless maintaining his research program, and the day before his last hospitalization, I was planning to drive him to Philadelphia so he could work on an academic paper with a colleague. At the wake before his funeral Mass, his mentor and friend, Dr. Moody Wharam, one of the pioneers of radiation oncology, said to me, and speaking for his Hopkins colleagues, "We just lost our next Nobel Prize."

He was an extraordinarily committed husband and father: he and my daughter shared a great marriage, packing a superabundance of love, devotion, and mutual support into five and a half years, and his joy in being "Daddy" to William was itself a joy to behold. And he was a man of faith, whose faith sustained his good humor, his clear-mindedness, and his determination during an illness about which he, a consummate young professional, knew all too much. That faith was matched by Gwyneth's; more than one friend, in the week before Rob died, described Gwyneth's strength and dignity as that of a biblical heroine. I am a suspect witness, of course, but I could not have agreed more.

When I put Gwyneth's hand into Rob's at the foot of the altar at St. Jane Frances de Chantal Church in Bethesda, Maryland, on August 16, 2004, the day of their wedding, I was able to get out three brief sentences before my throat tightened up and my eyes became misty: "You two are great. Be great for each other. Let Christ be great in you." Gwyneth and Rob were all of that, and more, as they finished medical school together, did residencies together, brought William into the world together, and felt the sword of sorrow pierce their souls together. All of that good lives on, I am certain—as I am certain that I shall pray for the divine assistance through my son-in-law's intercession until he reaches out to me as I cross the threshold of hope.

The Homeric Manager
Earl Weaver (1930–2013)

Given the divine sense of humor, the reception committee appointed to meet Earl Weaver when the Hall of Fame manager of the Baltimore Orioles during their dynasty years arrived at the Pearly Gates on the morning of January 19, 2013, might have been interesting.

It could, for example, have included Mike Cuellar and the first Mrs. Earl Weaver.

After the Orioles acquired him from the Houston Astros, Cuellar's less-than-overwhelming career took off and the screwballing Cuban nicknamed "Crazy Horse" reeled off four twenty-win seasons in six years while Weaver was chain-smoking Raleighs in the passageway behind the Orioles' dugout. But by 1976 Cuellar had lost it, and Weaver, who hated to cut veterans who had won for him, had to let him go. As such things often are, it was an unhappy separation, immortalized by Weaver's comment to an overly aggressive reporter whose questions seemed to imply a lack of loyalty on Earl's part: "I gave Mike Cuellar more chances than I gave my first wife."

Immediate postmortem commentary quickly focused on Weaver's legendary feuds with umpires (whose incompetencies, it should be noted, have increased since the days when managers like Weaver literally got into the arbiters' faces). Other baseball commentators noted that Weaver was a pioneer of sabermetric managing, keeping detailed notes on opposing pitchers and hitters long before the days of stat-loaded laptops in the dugout, so as to create the best situations for his own teams—a craftiness that made the careers of such platooned Orioles batsmen as John Lowenstein, Gary Roenicke, Benny Ayala, Terry Crowley, Lenn Sakata, and Joe Nolan, and that helped less-than-overpowering relief pitchers such as Tippy Martinez, Tim Stoddard, and Sammy (the "Throwin' Swannanoan") Stewart enjoy major-league success beyond what their talents might have foretold.

Still others noted that Weaver never cultivated close friendships with his players, which suggests that he would not have fared well in a psychiatric hothouse like the Boston Red Sox clubhouse has been known to be, even when the Carmine Hose were winning world championships. But this alleged aloofness seems a bit overdrawn.

Weaver liked eccentrics and the relaxed atmosphere their antics could create, which he believed helped men play a very hard game more easily. (As his longtime pitching coach, Ray Miller, once observed, you can't play baseball with clenched fists.) So he encouraged the postgame clubhouse kangaroo court over which Frank Robinson presided in a faux-periwig fashioned from a mop, at which players who had messed up in the game just completed were indicted, convicted, and fined—a buffoonery, Weaver understood, that cleared the air and prevented a warped kind of class consciousness from dividing his team. But he also encouraged individual craziness.

The aforementioned Sammy Stewart, for example, was a true nut who relished tweaking Weaver. For months, one season, the righthanded pitcher practiced throwing lefthanded, so that he could, when called into a game in a (presumably dire) relief situation, try a southpaw pitch, just to see what Weaver's reaction would be. After months of practice, Stewart was summoned from the bullpen one night, took his practice throws righthanded—and then turned on the mound and threw the batter a pitch from the port side. Weaver's reaction? Stewart later told a reporter, "Earl didn't let me down. He just said, 'That's why I like comin' to the ballpark every day. You never know what the hell you're gonna see.' "

Then there was catcher Rick Dempsey, who entertained hundreds of thousands during rain delays with his one-man vaudeville act, "Baseball Soliloquy in Pantomime", which involved a great deal of flopping around the rain-soaked infield tarpaulin on his pillow-enlarged belly (he would be named the most valuable player of the 1983 World Series, the year after Weaver retired). Dempsey and Weaver had notable screaming matches about pitch selection and other arcana, and Dempsey decided on a unique form of payback. One year, as Thomas Boswell reported, Dempsey let his hair and beard grow over an entire off-season and then pranced into the Orioles spring-training clubhouse in tennis gear, like something out of a drag show. "Who the [expletive deleted] is that and how the hell did he get into our clubhouse?" Weaver hissed, perhaps hoping that someone would clobber the invader with a Louisville Slugger. "It's your catcher, Mr. Genius," Dempsey trilled, before flouncing away. Weaver loved it, as he loved the other antics of "the only guy who plays in foul territory".

In retrospect, Weaver's real genius lay in his ability to get the most out of very disparate groups of players. He inherited a block-buster team in 1968—Frank and Brooks Robinson, Boog Powell, multiple twenty-win pitchers like Dave McNally and Jim Palmer—and drove them to three straight American League championships, winning the 1970 World Series. In the middle 1970s, Weaver made do with fewer future superstars on their way to Cooperstown (save Palmer), but the Orioles kept on winning until the next Hall of Famer (Eddie Murray) arrived, to be followed in 1982 by yet another (Cal Ripken, Jr., whom Weaver, brilliantly, switched from third base to shortstop, telling the rookie, "Just play short like you did in high school, kid"). The Orioles' 1982 end-of-season run was a death-defying act for the ages, as week after week they closed the gap on the Milwaukee Brewers with one hair-raising late-game rally after another. (That month-long rush led to another classic Weaverism: "We've crawled out of more coffins than Bela Lugosi.") The Birds lost the pennant on the last day of the season, which was the last day of Weaver's real managerial career (he foolishly came back from retirement for an unhappy season and a half later in the mid-1980s), but the pitch of emotion in old Memorial Stadium that final day will never be forgotten by anyone remotely involved in Baltimore baseball and its fortunes.

In mid-July of that magical season, the Orioles came to Seattle, where I was writing about the Mariners for the Seattle *Weekly*. Armed with my press pass, I approached the Earl of Baltimore as he was sitting in the dugout during batting practice and thanked him for what he had done over the last fourteen years for the team I loved. He growled something about "what's that to me?" and lit another Raleigh. After the game, I ventured into the visitors' clubhouse in the dreadful Kingdome, whose multiple inadequacies included being really unwelcoming to the visiting team's manager and coaches, who were all crammed into a holding pen the size of a living room in a modest Baltimore row house. The coaches (including Cal Ripken, Sr.) dressed out of high school lockers against one wall, while the visiting manager's "office" was an Army-surplus metal desk and chair that took up about 30 percent of the space in the room. The scribal brethren were packed in there like sardines, everyone wanting a chance to hear Weaver on his last visit to Seattle. And there, in his own lair, crumby as it was, he didn't disappoint. Buck naked, with a Schlitz in one hand and a Raleigh in the other, he held forth for what I remember as the better part of an hour, one story after another, while Ripken the Elder and the other coaches quietly dressed and slipped away into the Puget Sound darkness.

The next day, I described this amazing scene to Barry Goren, a friend and colleague who had learned his baseball in Brooklyn in the 1950s, which is about as good as learning it in Baltimore in that same Golden Age. So how was it with Earl, Barry asked? Well, I replied, I now know what it was like listening to Homer recite the *Iliad*. The only thing lacking was the philosopher's *chiton*. But draped or undraped (as he was in this instance), Earl Weaver, the pint-sized, volatile, umpire-baiting Number 4, was a man of parts and ideas who cared far more than he usually let on.

Mom

Betsy Schmitz Weigel (1914–2009)

*A tribute delivered at the Cathedral of Mary Our Queen,
Baltimore, on October 28, 2009.*

In the twentieth chapter of Luke's Gospel, Jesus admonishes the Sadducees, in a debate in the Temple, that the God of Abraham, Isaac, and Jacob is "not God of the dead, but of the living; for all live to him" (v. 38). As I noted when we buried Dad from this cathedral five years ago, that admonition is one biblical reason why the Catholic Church wisely discourages "eulogies" at Masses of Christian Burial. Like those who heard the Lord in the Temple in Jerusalem, and like the holy women who found an empty tomb on Easter Sunday morning (cf. Lk 24:5), we are not to seek the living among the dead. And the truth we have celebrated in this Mass is that Betsy Weigel—our mother, mother-in-law, grandmother, grandmother-in-law, great-grandmother, aunt, neighbor, and friend—is among "the living": she lives in the Risen Lord who claimed her for his own at her baptism, ninety-five and a half years ago; she now lives in the purifying presence and majesty of God in a way that we can only envy, if we ponder her circumstances and ours in the light of faith. The God of Abraham, Isaac, Jacob, and Jesus is God of the living. So, let us not look for the living among the dead.

Rather, let us give thanks this morning for all the good that came from Mom's extraordinary life, which was as rich in faith, hope, and love as it was rich in years. Let us reflect on what continues to live from this godly woman whom we commit to the earth today, knowing that, through the grace of Christ and his redeeming power, Betsy Schmitz Weigel is among "the living" as she has never been before in all those nine and a half decades.

It is almost impossible to imagine the world—and the Baltimore—into which William Joseph Schmitz and Estelle Hebner Schmitz brought their firstborn, Betsy, on March 9, 1914: Woodrow Wilson was a year into his first term as president and Pius X was in his last months as pope; crowned heads ruled in St. Petersburg, Berlin, Vienna, and Rome; Hitler was a shiftless, failed artist in Munich and Lenin an exile in Paris; Babe Ruth had not yet signed a major-league contract; only science fiction writers imagined the DNA double-helix, or six American landings on the moon, or the curative powers of a mold called "penicillin".

The last mayor of Baltimore to have been a Civil War veteran had died just a few years earlier. Cardinal Gibbons was in his thirty-seventh year as archbishop of Baltimore; a future archbishop and cardinal, Lawrence Shehan—who would one day startle my mother by giving her a kiss on the cheek before accepting a Manhattan at our home at 18 Murray Hill Circle—was learning Latin and Greek at St. Charles College, over in Catonsville. And the Orioles were playing minor-league ball—which was, I suppose, a preview of the unhappy Age of Angelos.

Rodgers Forge and Murray Hill, where Mom and Dad lived for fifty-three years, were farms, far beyond 25th Street, the city's northern boundary, which wouldn't be extended to its present position until after Mom celebrated her fourth birthday. Everything and everybody in Baltimore was segregated. Women didn't vote. And to move from a two-story to a three-story row house was a sign of having made it, at least among the German middle class from which the Schmitz clan sprung. Mores were different, too: Mom's parents were engaged for seven years before their wedding, while my grandfather earned his medical degree and finished his training.

Five months after Mom was born, European civilization imploded in the First World War, and the twentieth century began in earnest. Mom lived through that entire epoch—from the guns of August 1914 through the collapse of Soviet communism in 1991—and then lived for another decade and a half in the twenty-first century, which as an epoch began in 1991, as the twentieth century as an epoch really began in 1914. Her life spanned nine pontificates and sixteen presidencies, three world wars (counting the Cold War), an ecumenical council, the civil rights revolution, the contemporary women's movement, the Sixties, the pro-life movement, the Revolution of 1989, 9/11—and the loss of the Colts to that obscure town somewhere in the Midwest. At her death, America had traveled as far in time from her birth as the country had previously traveled from the first administration of President James Monroe to the day that Betsy Hebner Schmitz entered the world.

It was a remarkable run. And her longevity was matched by her originality.

Hard as it may be to imagine, at least for those who knew her in her immaculately dressed and groomed adulthood, Betsy Schmitz's first reputation in Baltimore was as an athlete: a basketball star in the days when it was six girls to a side, half of whom had to remain in the backcourt, and everyone had to pass or shoot after three dribbles; a field hockey star who, if legend has it right, was not averse to whacking an opponent across their padded shins. She later became what the old *Baltimore News-Post* styled, in a lengthy profile of her, a "career-girl"—a medical technologist. And then she met Dad, and the next half-century and more were devoted to him, to her children and grandchildren and great-grandchild, with singular, unflagging devotion.

Mom was [my brother] John's and my first evangelist: she taught us our prayers, helped us learn the *Baltimore Catechism*, helped us memorize the Latin responses that enabled us to become altar boys in this cathedral church, and drove us to serve the 6:45 A.M. Mass with grape jelly sandwiches in our bookbags for breakfast afterward. Her example of prayer, and Dad's, which was both profound and unobtrusive, left its mark; so did their patience with occasionally rambunctious sons, who later experienced the joys of raising teenagers themselves; and so did the noble Baltimore German habit of offering sauerkraut with the Thanksgiving turkey, a tradition which continues to the third and fourth generation.

If her family was the chief focus of Mom's energy, love, and commitment from her marriage in 1949 until John and I left the house in Murray Hill to find our own ways in the world, there were two institutional commitments that enlivened decades of Mom's life. She was devoted to the College of Notre Dame of Maryland, where she had studied from the fourth grade through her bachelor's degree (all at the same Homeland campus); and she had a particular devotion to her teacher, guide, and counselor, Sister Margaret Mary O'Connell,

S.S.N.D., the college's longtime president, who brought Mom onto the Notre Dame biology faculty after her graduation in 1935 and a brief graduate school stint at Columbia. Mom later became the president of the Notre Dame Alumnae Association, until my arrival in 1951 compelled a change of command.

And then there was this Cathedral of Mary Our Queen. After John and I began our own families—having each married a Notre Dame alumna—Mom continued to work for years at the Cathedral rectory, preparing the weekly bulletin, making sure the crab cakes were just right for then-Archbishop Keeler's post-installation reception, and giving tireless service to the parish and the priests she and Dad loved. It is a blessing that one of those priests, Monsignor Paul Cook, is able to celebrate this Mass of Christian Burial today, as he did for my father five years ago.

Through all of this, Mom's devotion to Dad was steady, steadfast, and generous. There were sorrows; and I'm sure the celestial equivalent of tears of joy were shed this past Sunday morning when Mom, having passed through the valley of the shadow of death, met the daughter she had never seen, my sister, Anne, who died hours after her birth in 1956. Mom cared lovingly for her own mother as Estelle Hebner Schmitz became infirm in her old age. And the care that Mom gave our grandmother was more than matched by the exquisite care given Mom by John and [daughter-in-law] Linda, and by [their children] David and Gregory and Alison, at their home in Calvert County these past two and a half years. Mom died with Linda holding her hand and praying the Rosary with and for her—and if that is not the textbook definition of that "good death" for which we were taught to pray, I cannot imagine what is. Then there were the difficult months before Dad's death five years ago; Mom was, mercifully, spared the suffering from Alzheimer's disease that he endured, but she endured it with him, and did so with the bravery that comes from faith.

Mom's long and fruitful life was abundantly touched by grace. The sacraments to which she brought her sons were the sustenance of her own Christian life. Her amazing vitality lives in those to whom she gave life through her love for Dad, as her faith lives through the love for Christ and his Blessed Mother she transmitted to her sons. That faith and love resonates down through the generations—an echo, perhaps, of an older, in some ways harsher, in other ways better, Baltimore that long ago ceased to be and will never be again.

As she now lives in Christ, who gave his life for her, so her life lives in this world in all the lives she touched, among family and friends. Love, Hans Urs von Balthasar taught us, is the most living thing that is. Mom probably never heard of Hans Urs von Balthasar; but she knew, and lived, that truth of the orders of creation and redemption long before the great Swiss theologian committed it to paper.

We do not seek the living among the dead. We know that Betsy Schmitz Weigel lives because her Redeemer lives. She lives now in the embrace of the divine love with which she was abundantly blessed in this world. And for this, we give praise and thanks to God the Father, through the Son, in the power of the Spirit. Amen.

Dad

George Shillow Weigel (1921–2004)

A tribute delivered at the Cathedral of Mary Our Queen,
Baltimore, on October 23, 2004.

Your Eminence; Your Excellency; Monsignor Cook; Reverend
Fathers; Brothers and Sisters in Christ:

Last night, when I got home from the vigil service, I found a copy
of a telegram sent to the Apostolic Nunciature in Washington waiting for me. Its contents suggest that it was intended to be shared with
all of you:

> I was deeply saddened to learn of the death of your father, George
> Shillow Weigel, and I assure you of my prayers for you and your
> family during this difficult time. I join you and all those present at
> the Mass of Christian Burial in commending the soul of this hus-
> band and father to the merciful love of our savior, Jesus Christ. To all
> who mourn George in hope of the resurrection, I cordially impart my
> apostolic blessing as a pledge of peace and strength in the Lord.
>
> IOANNES PAULUS PP. II
> [Pope John Paul II]

Just before Saint Luke tells the story of the disciples on the road to
Emmaus, the evangelist narrates the first events of Easter morning in
these striking terms: "On the first day of the week, ... [the women]
went to the tomb, taking the spices which they had prepared. And
they found the stone rolled away from the tomb, but when they
went in they did not find the body. While they were perplexed about
this, behold, two men stood by them in dazzling apparel; and as they
were frightened and bowed their faces to the ground, the men said
to them, 'Why do you seek the living among the dead?'" (24:1–5).

207

The Catholic Church discourages eulogies at the Mass of Christian Burial for precisely this reason: like the women who had followed the Lord from Galilee to Calvary, we, too, are not to seek the living among the dead. Eulogies typically focus on the past, on what has been. Eulogies are incomplete because they lead us to look among what is dead for someone who is living. And what we have celebrated in this Eucharist is the truth that George Shillow Weigel is among the living: he lives in the Risen Lord who redeemed him; he lives in the Christ from whom he was born again in baptism, eighty-three years ago in Columbia, Pennsylvania; he lives an awareness of the presence, the majesty, and the purifying mercy of God in a way that we can only imagine and envy. So, let us not look for the living among the dead.

Let us reflect, rather, on what all who have stood by Dad and Mom in fidelity and friendship during these past difficult months have taught us: that love is the most living thing there is. And let us pause briefly and think about all that lives from this good man. We commit him to the earth today, but we do that knowing that, through the redeeming power of Christ, he is among the living of whom the angels spoke to frightened women in a garden outside Jerusalem, two thousand years ago.

For the seven years I served as president of the Ethics and Public Policy Center, I was privileged to have Admiral Bud Zumwalt, the former Chief of Naval Operations, as my board chairman. Dad and Bud were contemporaries, one a reserve naval officer who graduated from the University of Pennsylvania, the other an Annapolis graduate, both of whom had served America and the cause of freedom in the Pacific. On one occasion I told Bud that Dad, who like others of his generation spoke very little about his service, had once made a mildly ironic comment about the wisdom of the United States Navy, turning an economics major into the commander of *APc-18*, a coastal patrol craft in the Philippines Theater, rather than using him in supply or management or something for which his education had prepared him. Bud laughed and said, "I bet your father never told you that they screened those reserve officers for qualities of leadership—and then assigned the leaders to command those ships."

Of course, Dad hadn't told me that. His leadership was of a piece with his other qualities: understated. (Which, given the personalities of his sons, proves, I suppose, that understatement is not genetically transmitted in the male line down the generations.) His commitment to this cathedral church, the seeds of which were planted when he took me to its dedication on a bitterly cold day in 1959, was understated; but it was enduring. His volunteer work, teaching reading to adult illiterates, or doing "Meals on Wheels", was understated; but he kept feeding the hungry until he was unable to do so any longer. Even his successful professional life was understated; yet one of his colleagues told me that Dad, in addition to being a skilled manager, was a terrific salesman. I expect that was because people knew they could trust him.

It's part of the received wisdom about dementia that, as other facets of a personality disappear, the core qualities or virtues of a person remain. That is what our entire family has seen in these past several months. What endured in Dad was what was deepest in him: his courtesy and gentlemanliness; his profound love for Mom; his Catholic faith. Now, we believe, all of that is being purified and perfected, so that Dad becomes the saint that he was baptized to be—the saint that all of us are called to be, for to be a "saint" is to be someone who can live with God forever and enjoy the experience. And that is our human and Christian destiny.

Over the past several months of Dad's illness, I know that I have, and I expect we all have, had occasion to ponder Saint Paul's words in 1 Corinthians: "Now we see in a mirror dimly" (13:12). That was certainly Dad's experience in these past weeks and months. But now, as the apostle assures us, he sees clearly, "face to face" (13:12): the faces of his grandparents and parents; the faces of his brothers; the face of my sister, Anne, with whom he has been reunited after almost fifty years.

That is the "seeing" that lies on the far side of all suffering for a Christian. Suffering is part of our Christian vocation. We cannot avoid it; we do not deny it. For in baptism we put on Christ, and the life of Christ leads inexorably to the Cross. There, on Good Friday, the eternal Son took all the world's suffering upon himself in a perfect act of obedience. And that perfect gift of self-sacrificing love was vindicated on Easter Sunday morning, when the angels asked the women, "Why do you seek the living among the dead?"

We cannot know all the good that has come into the world because of Dad's life and because he identified his suffering with the sufferings of Christ. We can know, and we can give thanks for, all the good that has come into our lives through the grace of Christ, as we walked with Dad and each other up the road to this particular Calvary.

At a time and in a culture where suffering seems an absurdity, and instant cures are recklessly promised by scientists and politicians alike, Dad's last months bore witness to the truth that suffering, offered to God in obedience and in identification with Christ, is redemptive. Through suffering, we become the kind of people who can live with God forever. And we thank God for the witness to that truth that Dad was and is for us.

The Boston College philosophy professor Peter Kreeft writes that our lives, our history, look different when we see them as *his*-story, as Christ's story and our participation in that story. In that perspective, Kreeft suggests, suffering is the bass note in a "harmony whose high notes are lost in heaven". And the heaven that is promised us is the heaven described by Saint John, in his exile:

> Then I saw a new heaven and a new earth; for the first heaven and the first earth had passed away, and the sea was no more. And I saw the holy city, new Jerusalem, coming down out of heaven from God, prepared as a bride adorned for her husband; and I heard a great voice from the throne saying, "Behold, the dwelling of God is with men. He will dwell with them, and they shall be his people, and God himself will be with them; he will wipe away every tear from their eyes, and death shall be no more, neither shall there be mourning nor crying, nor pain any more, for the former things have passed away." And he who sat upon the throne said, "Behold, I make all things new." (Rev 21:1–5)

That is the truth in which Dad lived his life: as a son; as a young naval officer; as a husband and father and grandfather; as a business-man and a volunteer.

That is the truth in which he gave his soul to God this past Tuesday night [October 19, 2004], the Feast of the North American Martyrs and the twentieth anniversary of the death of a modern martyr—another "George"—Father Jerzy Popiełuszko, the heroic Solidarity priest who spoke truth to power in communist-dominated Poland.

That is the truth in which Dad lives today.

We do not seek the living among the dead. We know that George Shillow Weigel, like his Redeemer, lives—and lives in the embrace of divine love.

Literary Brilliance, with a Caveat
Tom Wolfe (1930–2018)

When the great Tom Wolfe died on May 14, 2018—he of the Yale doctorate, the white suits, the spats, and the prose style as exuberant as his wardrobe—I, like millions of others, remembered the many moments of pleasure I had derived from his work.

My Wolfe addiction began on a cross-country flight in 1979, shortly after *The Right Stuff* was published. Always an airplane and space nut, I was fascinated by Wolfe's re-creation of the culture of America's test pilots and astronauts at the height of the Cold War. And there was that extraordinarily vivid writing, redolent of the New Journalism but somehow under greater disciplinary control. At one point I burst out laughing, scaring the daylights out of the elderly lady sitting next to me but not daring to show her the passage—it must have involved Pancho Barnes' Happy Bottom Riding Club, a saloon outside Edwards Air Force Base—that set me off.

After *The Right Stuff* got me going on Tom Wolfe, it was impossible to stop. The first half of *Radical Chic and Mau-Mauing the Flak Catchers*—Wolfe's scathing account of a reception thrown for the Black Panthers by Leonard and Felicia Bernstein—remains the quintessential smackdown of political correctness among the 1 percent cultural elites. *From Bauhaus to Our House* crisply explains why anyone with an aesthetic sense thinks something is seriously wrong with modernist architecture, and does so in a way that makes you laugh rather than cry (or scream).

Then there was Wolfe's first novel, *The Bonfire of the Vanities*. One of its chapters, "The Masque of the Red Death", takes its title from Edgar Allan Poe and with mordant humor dissects the vacuity of Manhattanites defined (and in some cases destroyed) by their grotesque, over-the-top consumerism. On rereading that stunning setpiece for the umpteenth time, the thought occurred that here was a far more effective polemic against materialism than anything ever issued by the Pontifical Council for Justice and Peace. *Bonfire* was also brilliant in skewering the destructiveness of New York's race hustlers, the obtuseness of a values-free media, and the fecklessness of too many politicians.

Asked once by the monks who run a prestigious prep school what they might do to disabuse parents of the notion that their sons were doomed if they didn't get into Harvard, Duke, Stanford, and the like, I suggested giving a copy of *I Am Charlotte Simmons* to the parents of every incoming senior. Wolfe's fictional tale of life on elite American university campuses in the twenty-first century is a sometimes-jarring exercise in the social realism practiced (a bit less brutally) by Dickens and Balzac. But *Charlotte Simmons*, like Wolfe's other fiction, has a serious moral core and an important cultural message. The young innocent, the brightest girl in a small town who makes it to an elite university, gets corrupted by stages. And her moral corruption is preceded by intellectual corruption—the class in which she's taught that there's really nothing properly called "the truth".

I do have one postmortem caveat to register about Tom Wolfe's oeuvre, which takes me back to *The Right Stuff* (and while we're on that subject again, forget the inane movie). The central figure in Wolfe's tale of aeronautical derring-do is Chuck Yeager, the man who first broke the sound barrier in the Bell X-1, and did so with a couple of broken ribs, which he managed in-flight with the aid of a sawed-off broom handle. Yeager was an extraordinary figure who never became a national celebrity because of the (absurd) news blackout surrounding the X-1 project, and Wolfe clearly wanted to pay tribute to him as an unsung American hero.

To do so, however, Wolfe seemed to think he needed a foil, and he cast astronaut Gus Grissom in that role: "Li'l Gus", the Hoosier grit lampooned as a bumbler to make Yeager look even better. And that was a grave disservice to the memory of Virgil I. Grissom, who did not mess up the second Mercury space flight (Wolfe's account notwithstanding), who was a masterful test pilot, and who gave his life for his country in the launchpad fire that consumed Apollo 1—which Grissom knew to be a deeply flawed spacecraft and had urged NASA to improve.

So with Tom Wolfe and Gus Grissom both having crossed what Wolfe once called the Halusian Gulp, I hope these two American patriots are reconciled. Because they both had the right stuff.

The Storyteller

Herman Wouk (1915–2019)

Around 2009 or thereabouts, a friend and colleague suggested that I write The Great Vatican Novel. I quickly declined, not just because the truth about life behind the Leonine Wall is often stranger than fiction (and more so since the suggestion was made), but because the idea of writing a novel terrifies me. Writing large books—no problem. Sitting in front of a keyboard or a pad of paper and making it all up out of my head—characters, plot, dialogue—is beyond my imagination.

Which is one reason why I was delighted to become friends with Herman Wouk, who died on May 17, 2019, after an extraordinarily productive literary life.

Having won the Pulitzer Prize for fiction with the 1951 bestseller, *The Caine Mutiny*, Wouk never took his foot off the authorial accelerator for more than a half-century thereafter, reaching the pinnacle of his popularity with two more World War II novels, *The Winds of War* and *War and Remembrance* (for which he subsequently wrote screenplays). But while fiction was on my mind when we first met, it wasn't on Herman's. He was writing a companion volume to his well-regarded introduction to Judaism, *This Is My God*, and the Librarian of Congress, James Billington, suggested to Herman that he might want me to brief him on developments in Jewish-Catholic relations since *This Is My God* was published in 1959.

So over lunch at Washington's Cosmos Club, Wouk and I spent an hour going over Vatican II's teaching on Judaism and its deepening by Pope John Paul II; the advances recently made in the Jewish-Christian theological conversation by Father Richard John Neuhaus, Rabbi David Novak, and an unofficial group of Jewish and Christian scholars; and what the official terrain of Jewish-Catholic dialogue might look like in the future. As both host and interrogator, Herman could not have been more gracious, so when we were having coffee

I decided to pop the question that had been on my mind from the outset: How on earth do you sit down and write a novel? And specifically, where did Captain Queeg, the principal character in *The Caine Mutiny*, come from?

Wouk didn't miss a beat. There had been several mutinies in the U.S. Navy during World War II (all in port, incidentally), and the author had gotten permission from the Pentagon to read the transcripts of the trials that followed. Herman certainly drew on his own naval experience in giving *The Caine Mutiny* its verisimilitude and its array of characters; but the captain of the fictional destroyer-minesweeper USS *Caine*, Philip Francis Queeg, "emerged" from the testimonies of various officers at the real trials, he said. OK, I replied, what about Armin von Roon, the aristocratic Wehrmacht general who gives readers the view from the other side of the hill in *The Winds of War* and *War and Remembrance*? The answer was about the same: from Wouk's extensive reading in the memoirs of German officers, von Roon "emerged".

It may sound simple. What was really at work here, though, was disciplined talent informed by considerable human insight and dogged research.

One of our last conversations reminded me of the regularity of Herman's Jewish practice. He'd had his publisher send me the proofs of his penultimate novel, *A Hole in Texas*, which anticipated nuclear physicists' discovery of the Higgs boson while lampooning scientific hubris and governmental craziness. I'd read the galleys in a single sitting and called the author on a Saturday evening, Washington time, to congratulate him. But I'd miscalculated sundown in California and the housekeeper who answered the phone said, very politely, "Mr. Wouk will be happy to take your call after the Sabbath."

Herman Wouk's gift for storytelling was matched by his seriousness, and it would not be a mistake to think that he imagined writing as a vocation. Shortly after a lot of America began watching the televised adaptation of *The Winds of War* in the early 1980s, he reflected on a deep irony of his craft: "It is the paradox of my career that, though I have won recognition as a creator of war literature, I regard war and the preparation for war as the primal curse now afflicting the human race. Some serious writers have understandably averted their eyes from the skull that grins at them from current events, so as to create art from their private preoccupations. I have looked straight at the grinning skull and written about it."

This gifted, purposeful storyteller died at 103, still writing. May he rest with his forefathers, in the bosom of Abraham.

ACKNOWLEDGMENTS

If there is one thing the Internet, the blogosphere, and social media should have taught humanity, it's that God invented editors for a reason. I've been privileged to work with many fine members of that guild, and I'm grateful for their having commissioned or improved these elegies and reminiscences: Joseph Bottum; the late Linda Bridges; David Brewster; Charles Cooke; Bill Dodds; Nicholas Frankovich; Katherine Howell; Roxanne King; Theodore Kupfer; the late Kay Lagried; Aaron Lambert; Mark Lasswell; Rich Lowry; Karna Lozoya; Jon Meacham; Carl Olson; the late Mike Potemra; Molly Powell; Fred Schwarz; Nick Tell; Mark Wright.

I am also grateful to Dr. Raphael Navarro-Valls for inviting me to reminisce about his brother, and to my wife, Joan, for suggesting the book's title.

Natalie Robertson of the Ethics and Public Policy Center staff did a fine job of assembling the manuscript, with help along the way from Mark Shanoudy; Natalie also found the photographs that grace the cover.

It's a pleasure to dedicate this book to my grandchildren, two of whom—Bryn Chiara McCarthy and John Paul Weigel—arrived on the scene while the book was being prepared. I hope these stories help them (and William Joseph Spaeder, Claire Catherine Spaeder, and Lucy Gianna Spaeder) learn a bit more about some interesting people, and about their Papa.

GW
October 22, 2020
Memorial of Saint John Paul II

SOURCES

The essays in this book were originally published in newspapers, magazines, online platforms, and a book. As indicated below, many of the essays first appeared in George Weigel's weekly column, The Catholic Difference, *which is syndicated throughout the English-speaking world by the Archdiocese of Denver. Each essay has been revised for this collection.*

Fouad Ajami: The Catholic Difference, September 10, 2014.

Peter L. Berger: *National Review Online*, July 1, 2017.

James H. Billington: *National Review Online*, November 25, 2018.

Lindy Boggs and Cokie Roberts: *National Review Online*, September 18, 2019.

Tycho Brahe: *The Catholic Northwest Progress*, September 21, 1979.

Robert J. Breskovich: *The Catholic Northwest Progress*, September 30, 1993.

Don J. Briel: *National Review Online*, February 16, 2018.

William F. Buckley, Jr.: The Catholic Difference, April 9, 2008.

Charles W. Colson: The Catholic Difference, May 16, 2012.

William C. Doherty, Jr.: The Catholic Difference, November 16, 2011.

Audrey Donnithorne: *Catholic World Report*, June 12, 2020.

Hugh Dowding: The Catholic Difference, September 9, 2015.

Avery Dulles, S.J.: The Catholic Difference, January 28, 2009.

Albert Einstein: *The Catholic Northwest Progress*, September 18, 1980.

Cass Elliott and Denny Doherty: The Catholic Difference, July 18, 2007.

William Farrow, Dean Hallmark, and Robert Meder: The Catholic Difference, May 27, 2915.

Francis X. Ford, M.M.: The Catholic Difference, July 27, 2011.

Bernardin Gantin: The Catholic Difference, July 23, 2008.

Francis Eugene George, O.M.I.: *National Review Online*, April 17, 2015.

Andrew M. Greeley: The Catholic Difference, July 3, 2013.

Václav Havel: The Catholic Difference, January 18, 2012.

Dietrich von Hildebrand: The Catholic Difference, November 26, 2014.

Lubomyr Husar, M.S.U.: *National Review Online*, June 5, 2017.

Henry J. Hyde: *First Things*, February 2008.

Henry M. Jackson: *The Weekly* (Seattle), September 7, 1983; *The Catholic Northwest Progress*, September 8, 1983.

Franz Jägerstätter: *The Catholic Northwest Progress*, November 27, 1980.

Pope Saint John Paul II ("Conviction Changing History"): *Wall Street Journal*, April 4, 2005.

Pope Saint John Paul II ("The Broadness of a Gauge"): *Newsweek*, April 10, 2005.

Max Kampelman: The Catholic Difference, May 8, 2013.

Leonard Klein: *Catholic World Report*, December 12, 2019.

Leszek Kołakowski: *National Review Online*, July 24, 2009.

Charles Krauthammer: The Catholic Difference, August 1, 2018.

Aaron Jean-Marie Lustiger: Essay commissioned for the website of the Archdiocese of Paris, 2007.

Paul V. Mankowski, S.J.: The Catholic Difference, September 16, 2020.

Gino Marchetti: The Catholic Difference, September 4, 2019.

John R. Miller: *National Review Online*, October 6, 2017.

Daniel Patrick Moynihan: The Catholic Difference, October 27, 2010.

Francis X. Murphy, C.Ss.R.: The Catholic Difference, May 29, 2002.

Jim Mutscheller: The Catholic Difference, April 29, 2015.

SOURCES 221

Joaquín Navarro-Valls: Essay commissioned for *Navarro-Valls, el portavoz: Testimonios de sus amigos*, ed. Rafael Navarro-Valls (Madrid: Ediciones Rialp S.A., 2019).

Richard John Neuhaus: *Newsweek*, January 12, 2009.

Michael Novak: *National Review Online*, February 17, 2017.

Jan Nowak-Jeziorański: The Catholic Difference, February 16, 2005.

Flannery O'Connor: The Catholic Difference, April 16, 2014.

Robert C. Odle, Jr.: *National Review Online*, December 2, 2019.

Arne Panula: *National Review Online*, April 15. 2017.

Robert Pickus: *National Review Online*, January 25, 2016.

Pioneer 10: *The Catholic Northwest Progress*, May 5, 1983.

Frank Robinson: *National Review Online*, February 9, 2019.

Jackie Robinson: The Catholic Difference, April 19, 2017.

Anwar Sadat: *The Catholic Northwest Progress*, October 29, 1981.

James V. Schall, S.J.: *National Review Online*, April 21, 2019.

Sophie Scholl: The Catholic Difference, March 14, 2019.

Pete Seeger: The Catholic Difference, February 12, 2014.

R. Sargent Shriver: The Catholic Difference, February 16, 2011.

Robert Charles Susil: The Catholic Difference, February 17, 2010.

Earl Weaver: *National Review Online*, January 22, 2013.

Betsy Schmitz Weigel: Tribute delivered at the Mass of Christian Burial, Cathedral of Mary Our Queen, Baltimore, October 28, 2009.

George Shillow Weigel: Tribute delivered at the Mass of Christian Burial, Cathedral of Mary Our Queen, Baltimore, October 23, 2004.

Tom Wolfe: The Catholic Difference, July 18, 2018.

Herman Wouk: The Catholic Difference, July 10, 2019.

PHOTO CREDITS

Peter L. Berger, photo by Adam Bielawski, 2011, https://commons.wikimedia
.org/wiki/File:Cardinal-Francis-George_110516_photoby_Adam-Bielawski.jpg.
Available under the Creative Commons BY-SA 3.0 unported license.

James H. Billington, photo by John Mathew Smith & www.celebrity-photos.com,
2000, https://www.flickr.com/photos/kingkongphoto/46147317375/. Available
under Creative Commons BY-SA 2.0 license.

Don J. Briel, photo by Umarymarketing, University of Mary, 2014, https://
commons.wikimedia.org/wiki/File:Dr._Don_J._Briel.jpg. Available under Creative Commons BY-SA 4.0 license.

Avery Dulles, S.J., photo courtesy of Fordham University.

Francis X. Ford, M.M., photo courtesy of the Maryknoll Mission Archives.

Bernardin Gantin, photo uploaded by Diwi, "Von Kardinal Gantin geschenktes
Foto", 2007, https://de.wikipedia.org/wiki/Bernardin_Gantin#/media/Datei
:Gantin_Portrait.jpg. Available under a Creative Commons BY-SA 3.0 license.

Francis Eugene George, O.M.I., photo by Adam Bielawski, 2011, https://com
mons.wikimedia.org/wiki/File:Cardinal-Francis-George_110516_photoby
_Adam-Bielawski.jpg. Available under the Creative Commons BY-SA 3.0 un-
ported license.

Václav Havel, photo by John Mathew Smith, 1997, https://flickr.com/photos
/36277035@N06/5113187134. Available under the Creative Commons BY-SA
2.0 license.

Henry Jackson, photo courtesy of the U.S. Senate Historical Office.

Pope Saint John Paul II, photo by Dennis Jarvis, 2013, https://www.flickr.com
/photos/22490717@N02/12727135684. Available under the Creative Commons
BY-SA 2.0 license. Used with permission.

Leszek Kołakowski, photo by Verhoeff, Bert/Anefo, 1971, https://commons.wiki
media.org/wiki/File:Leszek_Kolakowski_1971.jpg. Available under the Creative Commons BY-SA 3.0 Netherlands license.

Charles Krauthammer, photo courtesy of Daniel Krauthammer.

Aaron Jean-Marie Lustiger, photo © P. RAZZO/CIRIC.

Michael Novak, photo by Gareth Rockliffe, courtesy of Jana Novak.

All remaining photographs are available in the public domain.